GW01066340

Portraits in Music 1

David Jenkins

Callendar Park College of Education, Falkirk

Mark Visocchi

Notre Dame College of Education, Glasgow

Oxford University Press
Music Department, Ely House, 37 Dover Street, London W1X 4AH

ACKNOWLEDGEMENTS

We are grateful to the following for permission to reproduce copyright material:

Music extracts

Boosey & Hawkes Music Publishers Ltd. (*Billy the Kid* by Aaron Copland and *The Execution of Stepan Razin* by Dmitri Shostakovich); Chappell & Co. Ltd. and Warner Bros. Music, Los Angeles (*An American in Paris* by George Gershwin) © 1929 New World Music Corporation, Copyright renewed, All Rights Reserved; Oxford University Press (*Sinfonia Antartica* by Vaughan Williams, *Portsmouth Point* by William Walton, and text from the libretto of *Rigoletto* by Edward J. Dent); Novello & Co. Ltd. (*Enigma Variations* by Edward Elgar and quotations from Elgar's own notes on the *Variations*); Peters Edition, London, New York and Frankfurt (*Till Eulenspiegel* by Richard Strauss); G. Schirmer Ltd., London (*Washington's Birthday* by Charles Ives) Copyright © 1937, 1964 by Associated Music Publishers Inc., New York; Universal Edition (London) Ltd. (*Háry János* by Zoltán Kodály).

Illustrations

p.4 Mansell Collection; p.5 Reg Wilson; p.7 Q.E.D. p.8 English National Opera; p.9 (left) Mansell Collection; (right) Mary Evans Picture Library; p.10 Horst Heibling ZEFA; p.12 London Symphony Orchestra; p.13 Hungarian Embassy; p.14 Mansell Collection; p.16 (left) Madame Sarolta Kodály; (right) Radio Times Hulton Picture Library; p.17 Bodleian Library (3); p.18 Scottish Tourist Board; p.19 Radio Times Hulton Picture Library; p.20 Aerofilms; p.21 Radio Times Hulton Picture Library; p.22 Barnaby's Picture Library; p.23 Mansell Collection; p.24 Spanish National Tourist Office; p.25 (left) Christina Burton; (right) Popperfoto; p.26 (bottom) Popperfoto; p.27 Popperfoto; p.29 Popperfoto; p.30 (left) G. Norris; (top right) Novosti Press Agency; (bottom right) Mansell Collection; p.32 Novosti Press Agency; p.33 Novosti Press Agency; p.34 (left) Radio Times Hulton Picture Library; (right) National Portrait Gallery; p.35 Kobal Collection; p.36 (left) Kobal Collection; (right) CBS records; Q.E.D.; p.37 Radio Times Hulton Picture Library; p.38 Radio Times Picture Library; p.39 Radio Times Hulton Picture Library; pp. 40-43 Elgar Foundation Ltd.; p.43 Geoffrey Hopcraft; p.45 Elgar Birthplace; p.46 (left) Camera Press; p.46 (right) Western Americana Picture Library (3) and pp.47-49 (4); p.50 (left) Oxford University Press; (right) Mansell Collection; p.52 Radio Times Hulton picture Library; p.53 Mary Evans Picture Library; p.54 Mansell Collection; p.55 Popperfoto; p.57 (left) CBS New York; (centre) Mansell Collection; p.58 Western Americana Picture Library; p.60 (left) Mansell Collection; (right) Mary Evans Picture Library; p.62 Radio Times Hulton Picture Library; p.63 (left) Mansell Collection; (right) Royal Academy of Arts.

The drawings of instruments on pages 12, 28, 35 and 38 are by Constance Dear.

Text

Oxford University Press for extracts from Vaughan Williams' programme notes for *Sinfonia Antartica*.

TO CLAIRE LOUISE

© Oxford University Press 1979

First published 1979
Third impression 1981

ISBN 0 19 321400 8

By the same authors

Portraits in Music 2

Designed by Clive Barnes, DP Press Ltd, Sevenoaks
Photoset by Type Practitioners Ltd, Sevenoaks
Printed in England by West Central Printing Co. Ltd., London & Suff[

CONTENTS

NOTE TO THE TEACHER

Portraits in Music is a collection of background material to be used in conjunction with 15 pieces of music for listening. While the music has been chosen carefully for its liveliness and general appeal, the depth of treatment which it will receive will depend on the needs and abilities of the class. The books can be used with secondary school pupils of any age following courses in which music listening plays a part. They will be particularly useful supplementary material for pupils in their fourth or fifth year working for CSE and O level examinations, since the selection of pieces is representative of the various musical styles and forms studied. One or two commonly 'set' works are also included. Each piece is covered in units of 3-5 pages containing background information drawn from original sources, songs to sing with guitar accompaniments, notes on composers and their periods, suggestions for follow-up work, useful information about forms, styles, and instruments, numerous illustrations, and a quiz. A *Guide to the Music* with mainly single stave extracts is printed, so that the pupils can easily follow the main themes of·each work as they listen.

In general, the pieces illustrate the theme that people, places and events have been a source of musical inspiration to many great composers: the scoundrel character of Till Eulenspiegel, the romance of Scotland, the tragic journey of Captain Scott to the South Pole. *Portraits in Music* attempts to remove some of the traditional barriers which frequently exist between music and other subject areas of the curriculum in the secondary school such as visual arts, drama, literature, poetry, and social studies.

Resources required to make full use of *Portraits in Music* include recordings of all items listed on the Contents page. (A Discography is provided despite the fact that this, due to constant deletions, can prove more frustrating than helpful! The references are correct, to the best of our knowledge, at the time of going to press.) A score of Verdi's *Rigoletto* (published by Boosey & Hawkes or Ricordi) may be borrowed from most public libraries and is necessary to supply piano accompaniments; these are best played at the transposed pitches indicated in the music quotes. Perhaps simple guitar accompaniments would provide the most satisfactory backing to the folksong-type material quoted in Copland's *Billy the Kid* Suite and similar items.

DAVID JENKINS
MARK VISOCCHI
1979

Rigoletto

AN OPERA IN 3 ACTS

BY GIUSEPPE VERDI (1813-1901)

Giuseppe Verdi was the greatest Italian opera composer of the 19th century. Born near Parma, son of a village innkeeper, at one time he thought of becoming a priest, but he was more interested in church music than in performing his clerical duties. Once he was caught listening to the organ and the priest kicked him downstairs! He tried to win a scholarship to the Conservatory in Milan but was refused because he was told he lacked aptitude for music. He managed to study privately, supported by a grant from charity, and at 24 he returned to Milan with his first opera — now forgotten. 18 more followed, among them *Rigoletto*.

These works form what is known as Verdi's 'early' period as a composer; they are characterised by their tuneful, vigorous melodies and melodramatic plots.

In 1850, Verdi was asked by the Fenice Theatre in Venice to write an opera for performance in the following year. Verdi decided to base his opera on *Le Roi s'amuse*, a play by the French author Victor Hugo. This play had caused a sensation in Paris 20 years earlier, and had been withdrawn after only one performance. People were shocked because the villain, the corrupt King Francis I, triumphed over all the virtuous characters.

Venice in 1850 was under Austrian military occupation. When Verdi's **librettist** (see page 8), Francesco Piave, completed his text from Hugo's play it was immediately banned by the Austrian authorities. The official reason given was that the plot was 'revoltingly immoral and obscenely trivial'. The real reason was because the Austrians were unwilling to put on an opera which presented royalty in an unfavourable light or gave the public a chance to express feelings against the Emperor of Austria.

Eventually, an agreement was reached. Verdi and Piave made some

Playbill for the first performance of Rigoletto *in 1851*

'necessary changes' in the libretto while keeping all the drama of the basic plot. These were some of the changes: King Francis I became the Duke of Mantua, other characters were given different names, and Italy became the setting for the action instead of France.

THE MAIN CHARACTERS

The Duke of Mantua (tenor) — a rich and powerful, handsome, pleasure-loving young man; he pursues one girl after another, not caring in the least about the unhappiness he causes.

Count Monterone (bass) — an elderly nobleman whose daughter has been deceived by the Duke. He places a curse on Rigoletto.

Rigoletto (baritone) — the Duke's hunchbacked jester; an unpleasant character, constantly teased and insulted by the Duke's courtiers.

Gilda (soprano) — Rigoletto's daughter; she is kept locked up in Rigoletto's house, protected from the evils of the Duke's court.

Sparafucile (bass) — a professional assassin.

Maddalena (alto) — Sparafucile's sister; she helps her brother by luring victims to their remote inn.

ACT I

In the Duke's palace, a party is in progress. The Duke sings the aria 'Questa o quella.'

Questa o quella — Original Key: A♭

Allegretto [Lively but not too fast] — *con eleganza* [elegantly]

Shall I bind me_____ in pro-mi-ses ten-der To but one_____ of the beau-ties_____ that hov-er a-round____ me? Or the em - pire_____ to an-y sur-ren - der_____ Of my heart that beats____ for me and for all? In the
con brio [with spirit]
plea-sures of love I have drown'd____ me, Ev-'ry joy with new ar - dour pur-su - ing;_____ If to-day, one____ shall find her un - do-ing, Then to-mor-row, then to-morr-ow____ an-o-ther will fall,_____ Then to-morr-ow____ an-o-ther will fall.

Count Monterone enters. His daughter has been deceived by the Duke, whom Monterone now demands to see.

Rigoletto, the Duke's jester, mocks Monterone and, in angry reply, Monterone curses both the Duke and Rigoletto.

Rigoletto is terrified by Monterone's curse. On his way home from the party, he meets Sparafucile, an assassin, who offers to help Rigoletto to get rid of Count Monterone.

Meanwhile, the Duke has found his way into the courtyard of Rigoletto's house where he meets Gilda, Rigoletto's pretty daughter. The Duke introduces himself as a poor student, and in the love scene which follows, the Duke sings 'E'il sol dell' anima, la vita è amore!'

E' il sol dell' anima — Original Key: B♭

Andantino cantabile [At a moderate pace, in a singing style]

Love to the heart is the fair light of morning, The soul a - wakening and life a - dorning;

The Duke leaves and Gilda returns to the house.

The Duke's courtiers, wearing masks, arrive in the courtyard. They know that a pretty girl lives in Rigoletto's house and have followed Rigoletto home to find out where he lives. The courtiers tell Rigoletto that they plan to enter his neighbour's house and Rigoletto is persuaded to join in. He puts on a mask, and in the darkness fails to notice that the courtiers have also blindfolded him. He holds a ladder, but because of his blindfold does not see that the courtiers are climbing into *his* house. Rigoletto has been tricked into allowing the courtiers into his home. They kidnap Gilda, and Rigoletto discovers the truth only when he finds his daughter's scarf on the ground.

ACT II

Returning to the palace, the courtiers tell the Duke that they have brought Gilda to him and he goes to the room where she has been taken.

Rigoletto enters and anxiously looks everywhere for his daughter. He begs the courtiers to help him, but they are pleased to have their revenge for the jester's cruel taunts.

Gilda appears and, sadly, tells her father how the Duke has deceived her. Rigoletto swears vengeance on the Duke.

ACT III

Maddalena, Sparafucile's sister, in league with Sparafucile and Rigoletto, has lured the Duke to a deserted inn. The Duke enters and sings 'La donna è mobile'.

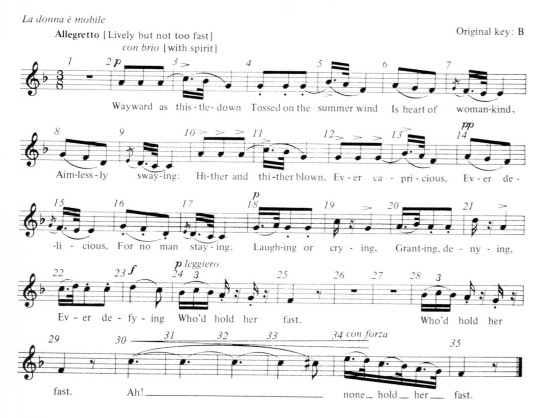

Gilda has been brought to the inn by her father who aims to prove to her how faithless the Duke is. (Gilda, incredibly, still loves him!)

Inside the inn the Duke serenades Maddalena with 'Bella figlia dell' amore'.

Then comes the famous Quartet as the Duke flirts with Maddalena inside the inn while, outside, Rigoletto and Gilda watch through a hole in the wall.

Maddalena, charmed by the Duke, persuades her brother to spare the Duke's life, and suggests that Sparafucile should murder the next person to arrive at the inn, handing over to Rigoletto the body in a sack as a substitute. Gilda overhears this conversation and, disguised as a man, decides to sacrifice herself. She knocks at the door of the inn and is stabbed by Sparafucile who does not recognise the woman in disguise.

Rigoletto returns at midnight to collect the body of the Duke and is handed the sack; while he gloats over the success of his plotting he hears the Duke's voice singing in the distance and, horrified, rips open the sack only to discover his own dying daughter. He collapses grief-stricken over her body with a cry of agony 'Ah! la maledizione!' The curse placed on him by Count Monterone has been fulfilled.

His present work is rather worse than better than previous productions by him. This opera is certainly not so noisy as *Ernani*, but it contains other grievous faults for which the mere absence of 'row' cannot compensate.

London Morning Post

We could not take it in at one hearing. The orchestration is admirable, marvellous; never was sound so eloquent.

Gazzetta di Venezia

Italian opera

In Italian opera, soprano, alto, tenor and bass voices are given traditional rôles in the casting of characters, e.g.

soprano — heroine/young girl
tenor — hero/young man
alto — older female characters/women who play minor parts in the operatic action, e.g. ladies' maids, gipsies
bass — the villain of the piece/high priest

Characteristic points of style in Italian opera include:

(a) relegation of the orchestra to the rôle of accompanist — this is singers' music
(b) severe demands are frequently made on vocal technique
(c) love duets are sung in sweet-sounding parallel melodic intervals of 3rds and 6ths
(d) division of the music into 'set pieces' rather than a continuous flow

Well-known 19th century composers of Italian opera include:

Rossini (1792-1868):
William Tell, Barber of Seville, Cinderella

Donizetti (1797-1848):
Don Pasquale, Lucia di Lammermoor, Daughter of the Regiment

Bellini (1801-1835):
Norma, I Puritani, La Sonnambula

Puccini (1858-1924):
Madame Butterfly, Tosca, La Bohème

Some 'set pieces' of Italian opera

Recitative

Recitative carries forward the action of the opera plot rapidly with the words of the text sung more or less in free speech rhythm and with only a relatively simple orchestral accompaniment to support the singer(s).

Aria

The aria (Italian word for 'song'), much more than recitative, tends to reflect characters' feelings about the situations they find themselves in. It is frequently in **ternary** form, i.e. in three parts with the third a repeat of the first (ABA). The aria is generally more elaborately accompanied by the orchestra.

Chorus

The chorus (male, female, or mixed) is generally made up of characters who are less directly involved in the action of the drama. They may be a crowd, an army, citizens or slaves, commenting on or taking part in the action. Very often, in the operas of Verdi, they represent the Italian people fighting for their freedom from Austrian rule.

Duet/Trio/Quartet

These are ensembles for two, three, or four characters respectively. The main challenge to the composer is to preserve the individual identities of the characters while maintaining an overall musical unity.

Libretto

The libretto is the text of an opera set to music by the composer. The **librettist** and the composer may be different (e.g. Verdi and Piave) but may be the same person. Wagner wrote his own libretti, as has done the contemporary English composer Sir Michael Tippett. Since it takes approximately 5 times longer to sing words than to speak them, adaptations of existing plays and new libretti must be correspondingly shorter than one might expect for a three-act opera.

Rigoletto and his daughter Gilda, played by Neil Howlett and Lois McDonall — *from a recent English National Opera production*

⇨ FOLLOW UP

Musical characterisation in opera

1. Listen to the Duke of Mantua's arias. Notice how light-hearted and melodious they are. In these Verdi has attempted to sketch, in music, the Duke's smooth manner, easy character, and attractive appearance by writing tunes which are equally smooth and irresistible. Listen to Gilda's aria, 'Caro nome'. Do you think Verdi's music succeeds in describing her beauty, grace, and innocence?

2. Listen to the melodies sung by Rigoletto; he's not a comic character nor an evil one — he is a tragic figure. What qualities (e.g. sadness, bitterness) can you find in Rigoletto's music?

3. How does Verdi portray the characters Sparafucile and Maddalena in music?

4. Finally, listen again, carefully, to the Quartet from Act III, one of the great ensembles in the world of opera. In the opening bars of the Quartet, given on page 6, note how the composer provides suitably contrasting melodies for the different characters: the Duke's is melodious while Maddalena's is teasing and mischievous; Rigoletto's music is solemn, while Gilda's is one of youthful heartbreak.

Till Eulenspiegel

TONE POEM

BY RICHARD STRAUSS (1864-1949)

Richard Strauss was born at Munich in 1864 and died at Garmisch-Partenkirchen in 1949, aged 85. He had two of his musical compositions published at the early age of 10, and went on to study at Munich and Berlin, but he first became known to the musical public as an orchestral conductor. He wrote operas, concertos, marches, serenades, songs, sonatas, and quartets, but is perhaps best known for his **tone poems** (see page 12), of which *Till Eulenspiegel* is the most popular.

Richard Strauss and his wife in 1914

Till Eulenspiegel lived in Germany in the 14th century. He was a shoemaker by trade and, more significant, an incurable practical joker. A restless good-for-nothing, he wandered around Europe earning a livelihood by trickery and deception and died of the Black Death at Lübeck in 1350. Many tales were told of his adventures and these legends were set down in print in the 15th century by a Franciscan friar from Strasbourg.

Till's childhood

Till grew up in the small village near Brunswick, where he acquired a bad reputation on account of his pranks and rudeness. Any stranger travelling through the village would find himself a long way from his correct route if he asked Till for directions. Till's parents, at first, were unaware of their son's tricks. His father, out on horseback with Till seated behind him, would be puzzled by his neighbours shaking their fists as he rode by — he could not see his son who, with his tongue out and his fingers wiggling from his hands stuck into his ears, was making faces at the people who passed by. Over the years

Old print of the city of Prague

Till's parents had so many complaints about their son that they decided to send him away from the village to learn a trade. With a bundle of clothes and a supply of food to last him several days, Till set out on his travels.

Till in Prague

In the city of Prague, Till, putting on a long white beard and a large pair of spectacles, introduced himself to the university professors as a famous scholar from Germany. He declared that he could answer any questions put to him. He was asked: 'How many gallons of water are there in the sea?', to which

he replied: 'Five hundred and ninety million, six hundred and twenty thousand, one hundred and thirty-seven gallons and a pint and three-quarters. If you do not agree, stop all the rivers and lakes from flowing into the sea and I will measure it for you'. Who could prove him wrong? Someone asked: 'How many days have passed since Adam's time to the present?' Till answered: 'Only seven days have passed and only seven can pass — Sunday, Monday, Tuesday, Wednesday, Thursday, Friday, and Saturday. If anyone can think of an eighth day, he is indeed a wise man!' Yet another question: 'Where is the middle of the earth?' Declared Till: 'I am at this very moment, standing over the middle of the earth — if you don't believe me, take a long string and make the measurement yourself!' The professors then began to argue among themselves about Till's replies. As the argument developed and grew more heated, Till, at a discreet distance, took off his false beard and spectacles, pulled a face at the angry professors, and then made a swift exit.

Till and the Prince of Marburg

Till often dressed in other disguises. One of his favourite tricks was to dress up as a monk and beg for charity. In Marburg, dressed as an artist, he agreed to paint the Prince of Marburg's portrait for a large sum of money. For days he stood in front of the canvas pretending to paint. At last, he announced that the portrait was finished. Till declared that only the most

Monument to Till Eulenspiegel at his birthplace near Brunswick, Germany

important citizens were allowed to view his finished masterpiece but of course they did not like to admit that the canvas was blank for fear of proving themselves unworthy to see it. The Prince himself was full of praise for the non-existent painting, and rewarded Till with a large sum of money.

Till and the peasant women

Among Till's favourite 'victims' were old peasant women who kept stalls in market places. One day he saw one of these women selling two hens and a cock in a basket. Till asked the price for the basketful of poultry and was told two silver pieces. Pretending to be a duke's servant, Till persuaded the woman to let him take the two hens in the basket, leaving her the cock, which she would give him when he returned with money from the duke! The bewildered woman agreed and, with the cock on her lap, sat down to wait. She is probably sitting there still — waiting for the rogue to return.

His death

When he died, Till was buried at Mölln, near Hamburg, where his tombstone can still be seen. As his coffin was lowered into the grave, the rope fastened to one end of it broke and his coffin came to rest on one end. And that was the way he was buried! A stone was placed over his grave and carved on it were these words:

From this stone keep all knavish hands
For Till below still upright stands!

GUIDE TO THE MUSIC

The piece opens with a short 'Once upon a time there lived a rascal' melody.

A French horn plays a suitably elusive melody which hints at Till's presence.

This melody is repeated, then, following a short pause, we come face to face with Till himself.

Beginning at this point in the piece, these two melodies are repeated in whole or in part, throughout the tone poem — listen for them.

Till's tricks begin. He rides through the market place, scattering pots and pans on the stalls and throwing the market women into confusion (listen to their screams on flutes and oboes!).

At once, he is off to new adventures in 'seven league boots'.

Next, disguised as a monk, Till preaches to the faithful.

But his mockery of religion suddenly weighs heavily on his conscience and, in terror, his knees knock together.

Till escapes — solo violin glissando. (Look at the list of Musical Terms at the front of the book if you don't know what this means.)

Till now plays the cavalier, romancing with the girls, first as a jest — and then seriously,

but the lady scorns him, and his anger and frustration are vividly portrayed by the orchestra, Till goes off, determined to avenge himself.

Till finds himself among learned scholars (remember the story and Till's questions?). The academic bearing of these gentlemen is amusingly suggested by the lower woodwind.

Till's questions are discussed by the scholars, each one taking up the subject in turn — the instruments seem to snatch the tune from one another as the discussion develops: at the height of the argument there is a sustained orchestral trill — Till decides he has endured enough pedantry for the day and, whistling a vulgar little tune, he quits the company.

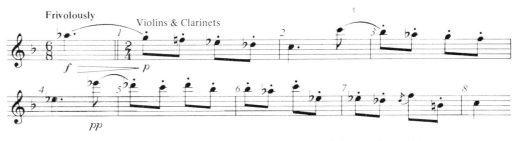

From now on Till's pranks take on a recklessness which is reflected in the music as it builds up to a climax, where a sudden break presents a terrifying roll on the side-drum — Till has been arrested.

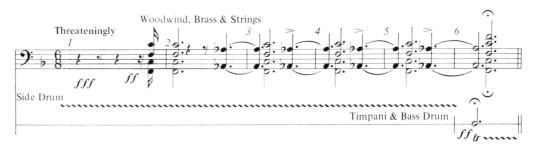

Till is brought before a judge.

Till's appeals (in short solo clarinet passages) go unheeded. The judge reminds him of his past misdemeanours (the orchestra making appropriate musical references to these former pranks).

After waiting for a few anxious moments, Till's sentence is given.

The solemn descent from the brass instruments tells us that Till has met his end on the gallows. A last gasp from clarinet and flute completes the scene.

A short epilogue opens with the 'Once upon a time' melody and concludes with a last laugh from Till — he lives on in the tales of his adventures!

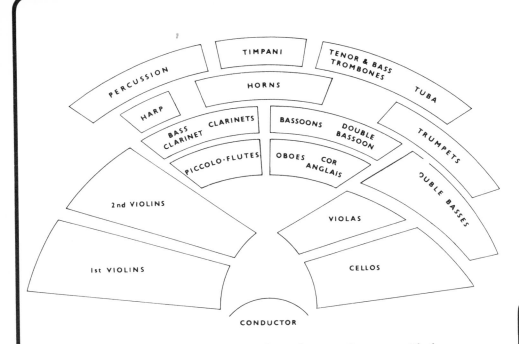

The London Symphony Orchestra taking a bow after a performance with the conductor André Previn

Programme music

Strauss's tone poem *Till Eulenspiegel* was first performed on 5 November, 1895, in Cologne. It attempts to relate in musical sounds incidents from Till's notorious 'career' and so comes into the category of **programme music** in which a composer tries to convey non-musical ideas, e.g. a picture or a story, in musical terms. This tone poem is scored for large orchestra, and the music, in addition to picturing many of Till's pranks, gives us a character-sketch of the rascally hero.

☞ *FOLLOW UP*

1. Listen to *Till Eulenspiegel* again and point to the section/sections of the orchestra which you think is/are most prominent as you go. Do this on your own, and your teacher will check if you are pointing at the correct section(s).

2. Till's theme is played by the French horn in Strauss's piece.

Find out what you can about
(a) how sounds are produced using the lips, and
(b) the use of valves on this difficult instrument.
You will find information in a music dictionary or a book on instruments.

The French horn

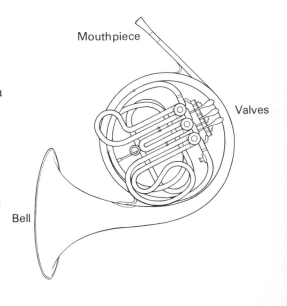

Háry János

ORCHESTRAL SUITE

BY ZOLTÁN KODÁLY (1882-1967)

Kodály with Hungarian school children on his 80th birthday, 16 December 1962

Zoltán Kodály was born in Hungary in 1882 and studied at the Conservatory of Budapest. He was particularly interested in the folk music of his own country, and along with his fellow Hungarian, Béla Bartók, collected folk tunes. Besides *Háry János*, Kodály wrote two other operas, many choral works, songs, piano and chamber music, some orchestral works, and music for schools, many of his compositions being inspired by his native country.

Háry János (we should call him János Háry, but Hungarians put the surname first) was a real character who fought in the Napoleonic wars, and Kodály used his legendary adventures on which to base the story line for his folk-opera *Háry János*. The orchestral suite, in six movements, contains music from the opera.

I. Prelude: The Fairy Tale Begins

The background to the music is a village inn where Háry János is boasting about his imaginary adventures.

As it begins there is a tremendous 'sneeze' from the orchestra to show that everyone knows to take the stories with a pinch of salt. (Hungarian superstition says that if a storyteller sneezes while he is speaking he must not be taken too seriously!) This orchestral 'sneeze' is represented by a violent upward rush of strings and woodwind, followed by a downward glissando on the piano accompanied by a long drum-roll.

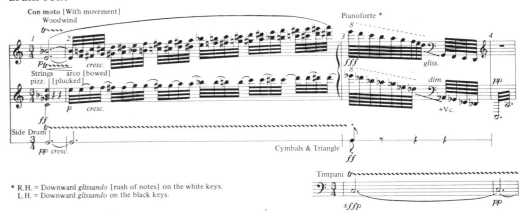

* R.H. = Downward *glissando* [rush of notes] on the white keys.
L.H. = Downward *glissando* on the black keys.

First, he tells how, once, when he was a Hungarian hussar on guard at the frontier of Russia and Hungary, he rescued the Empress Marie Louise, wife of the French Emperor, Napoleon. She was in the guardhouse on the Russian side of the frontier, and would have had to stay there at least a week until a high official came to let her out. But Háry János simply lifted the whole house bodily to the Hungarian side of the frontier, and she was free! She thought that he was the most handsome, bravest, and strongest man she had ever met and insisted on taking him to be one of the bodyguard of her father, the Hungarian Emperor in Vienna.

As János talks the Prelude continues in tranquil mood, with double basses and cellos murmuring a theme which is taken up by bassoons, clarinets, violins, flutes, and horns.

The music becomes passionate as János warms to his tale, and then the brass instruments take over this theme before transferring it back to the strings. The movement ends with the flute and clarinet playing a fragment of the theme against chords from the horns.

II. Viennese Musical Clock

At the Emperor's palace János found a garden with trees of gold and flowers in the shape of crowns (so he said). He saw the double-headed Austrian eagle, each head being fed with chickens, and a gigantic mechanical clock. The Empress herself, he said, took a fancy to him and showed him how it worked. When the clock struck, out came a row of clockwork soldiers dressed in all the various uniforms of the Imperial Army.

This movement is scored for woodwind, brass, piano and percussion; tubular bells, gong, celesta, triangle, cymbals, and the piano give the effect of the bells and chimes.

Listen for the marching tune of the clockwork soldiers.

At the end of the row was a Hungarian hussar. This did not suit Háry János at all; he insisted that the hussar was the best of them all and ought to come first. 'Oh, certainly!' said the Empress. 'I'll have it altered at once'.

III. Song

Háry János' Hungarian sweetheart, Ilka, who has followed him all the way from their native village, was rather disapproving of all this grand life at court and jealous of the Empress's interest in János. But he assured her that he only cared for her and longed for the time when they both could go back to Hungary. They felt nostalgic, and Ilka sang a sad Hungarian song.

The theme of this movement is a Hungarian folk-song, played first on the solo viola.

Then follow variations on the tune, and you will hear the Hungarian cimbalom with its characteristic 'twangy' tone. You can find out more about this instrument on the next page.

IV. The Battle and Defeat of Napoleon

Warning came that Napoleon, the husband of Marie Louise, had declared war on the Emperor of Hungary, and was going to attack immediately, with his French army. János was, of course, quite unafraid. He handed his pipe to a soldier, and said, 'Just take that while I go and deal with them!' A French military band entered, dressed in the most remarkable uniforms and blowing fantastic wind instruments. Everyone waited while they played their march, scored for piccolo, brass, and percussion.

A soldier trying to capture Napoleon's standard

Then Háry János swung his enormous sabre and the wind from it knocked the players over on their faces — dead! At this point Napoleon himself came on the scene, looking exactly like his portraits, only much larger. On seeing János he stopped suddenly. 'Háry János!' he gasped, and fell on his knees, immediately giving up his sword. Háry commanded the remainder of the French army to carry off the dead; they all stole away and Napoleon tried to hide behind a cannon. Marie Louise disowned her husband, thinking that he was a coward, and determined to marry Háry János instead.

Notice that the saxophone tune in the funeral march is the same as the swaggering marching tune, but with all the perkiness gone from it:

The mournful tones of the tubas and the doleful saxophone melody give a delightful musical caricature of Napoleon's downfall.

V. Intermezzo

In the opera this is played between the acts. Kodály uses a gipsy tune for the main theme with a characteristic rhythm found in many Hungarian tunes. The cimbalom is again heard ornamenting the melody.

The middle section has a more peaceful melody, played first by the horn.

VI. Entrance of the Emperor and his Court

The war was over. Marie Louise took Háry János back to Vienna to make her husband, and her father, the Emperor, gave a feast in his honour.

There is a feeling of oriental splendour about this last movement with its rich orchestration and march rhythm.

However János behaved very badly at the meal, finding fault with the food and throwing it about. In the end he decided he would rather marry Ilka and live in his own little village than stay in Vienna.

The scene returns to the inn, and Háry says, 'Well, that's how I captured Napoleon, and almost became the Emperor's son-in-law'. The listeners agree with a nod (and a wink) that everybody knows that Háry János is the greatest hero in the world!

The cimbalom

You will have noticed the unusual orchestral sound of the cimbalom used in the 'Song' and the 'Intermezzo'. Frequently used by Hungarian gipsies and in dance bands, Kodály incorporated a part for it perhaps to stress the folk-element of the story. The instrument is a kind of dulcimer with horizontal strings which are played with small wooden hammers — like a piano minus mechanism!

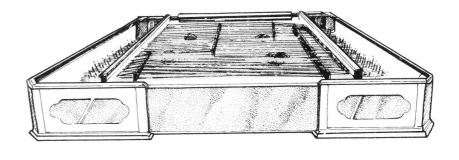

Nationalism in music

Kodály, like his friend and fellow composer, Bela Bartók, collected Hungarian folk-tunes, and this interest in his native culture spread over into his own composing style through the use of national folk rhythms and instruments. This trend towards nationalism in music was part of a more general move in this direction in countries as widely spread in Europe as Finland (Sibelius), Bohemia (Smetana) and Spain (de Falla) towards the end of the 19th century.

Bartók with Kodály (on the right) in 1912

Hungarian peasants

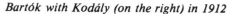 FOLLOW UP

Having listened to Kodály's musical imitations of a Viennese musical clock, what about making up your own 'clock-music' using some tuned and untuned percussion instruments? Organise your activity using the following simple score, and experiment to find the best ways of playing the instruments. Your teacher will help you. The score is divided up into blocks of 5 seconds which you can measure using a watch.

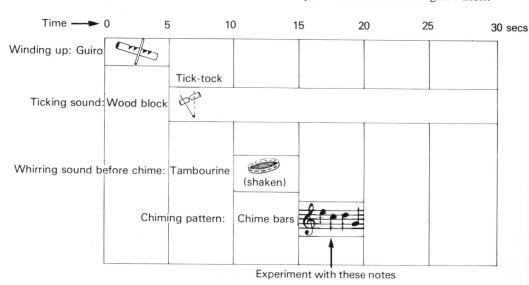

Experiment with these notes

16

Symphony No. 3 in A minor (Scotch)

BY FELIX MENDELSSOHN (1809-1847)

Edinburgh — from Mendelssohn's sketch book

In April 1829, Mendelssohn wrote to his friend Carl Klingemann in London:

Next August I am going to Scotland, with a rake for folksongs an ear for the lovely, fragrant countryside, and a heart for the bare legs of the natives.

Klingemann, you must join me; we may lead a royal life! Demolish the obstacles and fly to Scotland.

Before journeying to Scotland Mendelssohn had just had a triumphant season in London, during which he had been acclaimed as a virtuoso pianist, composer, and orchestral conductor.

He and Klingemann made the journey up the Great North Road to Edinburgh, arriving in the Scottish capital on 26 July after a week's trip by coach.

On his travels Mendelssohn kept a sketch book in which he drew pictures of places and events which captured his interest.

In Edinburgh he was impressed with the sights and sounds of the city and its history; soon he formed the idea of composing a 'Scotch Symphony'. On 30 July, in the ruined chapel of Mary Stuart in the Palace of Holyrood, Mendelssohn found inspiration for the introduction to the first movement.

Felix Mendelssohn was born in Hamburg, the son of a wealthy banker. Musically he was a child prodigy, and before he was 15 he had composed many symphonies and an opera. He was encouraged by his father to travel abroad, and his first important tour brought him to Scotland in 1829.

In the evening twilight we went today to the Palace where Queen Mary lived and loved. A little room is shown there with a winding staircase leading up to the door. Up this way they came and found Rizzio (Mary's secretary and supposed lover) in the little room, pulled him out and three rooms off there is the dark corner where they murdered him. The chapel close to is now roofless; grass and ivy grow there; and at the broken altar, Mary was crowned Queen of Scotland. Everything around is broken and mouldering, and the bright sky shines in. I believe I found, today, in that old chapel the beginning of my Scotch Symphony.

Although the Scotch Symphony was begun in 1829 it was not in fact completed until 1842. On his first visit to Buckingham Palace in that year Mendelssohn obtained Queen Victoria's permission to dedicate the work to her, and the visit to the Palace began a friendship with Victoria and Prince Albert (both keen amateur musicians) which lasted for the remainder of the composer's life.

The coach in which Mendelssohn and Klingemann travelled to Edinburgh — from the composer's sketch book

GUIDE TO THE MUSIC

FIRST MOVEMENT

Andante con moto [With leisurely movement]
Woodwind, horns & lower strings

The music of the introduction to the first movement rises to a climax before subsiding into a partial repetition of the opening theme. This leads to the main section of the first movement; its hushed first theme is scored for clarinet and strings alone.

Allegro un poco agitato [Lively, slightly agitated]
Clarinet and strings

Soon a contrasting theme is heard on the clarinet.

Allegro un poco agitato

Note how the melody played against the clarinet tune is based on the opening tune of this section, and try to hear these two tunes as independent lines which fit together perfectly.

Mendelssohn goes on to develop these musical ideas and the music proceeds through varying moods: at times warlike, tender, or sorrowful — but always agitated. The intensity builds up to a storm-like passage before the return of the opening *Andante* theme to round off the movement.

SECOND MOVEMENT

The most direct reference to Scotland in the symphony occurs in the second movement. In this fleet-footed *Scherzo* (Italian for 'joke') Mendelssohn uses a theme built on the five-note scale characteristic of all bagpipe music, and the tune ends with the little rhythmic 'snap' which is also a feature of Scottish folk music.

Vivace non troppo [Lively, but not too fast]
Clarinet

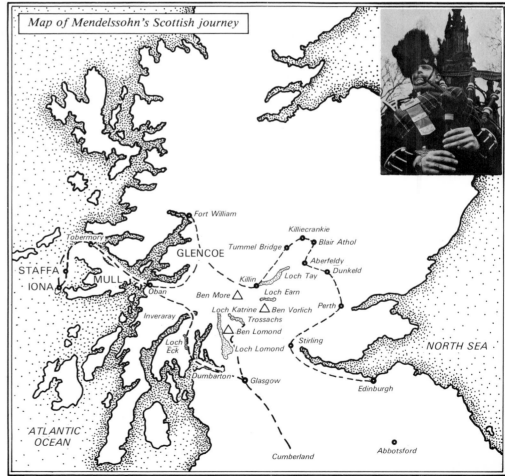

Map of Mendelssohn's Scottish journey

THIRD MOVEMENT

Nine introductory bars lead to the slow movement of the symphony. The poignant, intensely melodic slow movement could well be a further reflection on the ill-fated Queen Mary Stuart.

Mendelssohn alters the mood of the music by introducing an almost military tune, the rhythm of which has already been suggested by the horns in the nine introductory bars to the movement.

This tune occurs three times between varied orchestrations of the first tune and each time in a different key.

Near the end of the movement the broken phrases of the first tune played on the clarinet, quietly punctuated by references to the military rhythms, sound rather like a warrior's sad farewell.

FOURTH MOVEMENT

The last movement (or finale) of the symphony brings back a sterner mood. It might suggest a wild highland fling, a gathering of clan chiefs, and so on. Think about a film or a TV play you might have seen about the 'gathering of the clans' or other similar situation, and you will really enjoy this movement. There are two clearly recognisable themes.

The last movement of the symphony ends with a majestic *Allegro*.

Mendelssohn playing before Queen Victoria and the Prince Consort, by C. Rohling

The symphony

There are normally four movements in a symphony:

I A fast movement (in 'sonata form') — often marked *allegro*
II A slow, song-like movement — often marked *andante* or *adagio*
III A dance-derived movement (usually a minuet or *scherzo*)
IV A fast movement (finale) — often marked *allegro*

The first movement of a symphony is usually in what is known as **Sonata Form**, so-called because this is the form in which first movements of Sonatas (works for solo instruments) were often written. Mendelssohn's first movement follows this pattern. Listen to it again and see if you can spot how it fits into typical Sonata Form.

1. A slow, impressive introduction.

2. EXPOSITION. Two contrasting themes: the first (called the FIRST SUBJECT) in the tonic or main key of the movement, the second (called the SECOND SUBJECT) in the dominant key (i.e. the fifth note of the scale). A 'rounding off' passage leads to the

3. DEVELOPMENT. This section 'develops' the themes of the Exposition, i.e. the composer is free to vary any of the following elements of the themes — melody, harmony, rhythm, orchestral scoring. The development is followed by the

4. RECAPITULATION (or 'repetition'). Both the themes of the Exposition are heard again, but this time the second is also in the main key of the movement. This leads into the

5. CODA (Italian for 'tail'). A concluding passage to the movement.

Fingal's Cave from the air

☞ FOLLOW UP

1. One of the places that made a profound impression on Mendelssohn was Fingal's Cave on the island of Staffa. A small, bare, rocky, uninhabited island which lies off the west coast of Mull, Staffa is one of the many islands known as the Hebrides, and the Atlantic waves have carved a cave out of the black volcanic rock. Listen to a performance of Mendelssohn's **concert overture** *Fingal's Cave* and discuss to what extent you think the music matches the mood of the place he visited. (An **overture** is a piece of music played at the beginning of a play or an opera. A **concert overture** is a dramatic piece specially written for performance in the concert hall. See page 53.)

2. These words are all connected with Scottish music: **drone, mouth music, snap, bagpipes.** Write a few lines about each.

Suite Española

BY ISAAC ALBÉNIZ (1860-1909)

Isaac Albéniz was born in the part of Spain called Catalonia. He led an adventurous early life: he was only four when he gave his first public recital. Three years later, having failed to gain admission to the Conservatory of Paris because of his age, he was accepted as a student at the Conservatory of Madrid.

When Albéniz was nine he ran away from home to give recitals all over Spain, then stowed away aboard a ship bound for Puerto Rico and worked his

passage by providing musical entertainment for the passengers. On arrival in America he organised single-handed a recital tour which took him from Cuba to San Francisco.

At 13 he returned to Europe and until the age of 30 travelled widely giving piano recitals. Thereafter he dropped playing in favour of composing music, mainly for the piano and often based on the folk music of his native country.

To most people Spanish music suggests flamenco guitar music and gipsies dancing to the strain of the habañera. They might also think of the many attempts at composition in the Spanish idiom by composers from other countries, for example, in Bizet's *Carmen*, Rimsky-Korsakov's *Spanish Caprice*, Chabrier's *España*, and Ravel's *Bolero*. These, however, give little idea of the vast range and contrasts to be found in real Spanish folk music.

In his *Suite Española* Albéniz takes us round the different parts of Spain and introduces us to the variety of music which accompanies the dances from different regions. (Find them on the map on page 24). In doing so he succeeds in capturing the essence of Spanish music in a way which no other

composer has matched. Albéniz's suite of piano pieces has been colourfully orchestrated by Rafael Frühbeck de Burgos, a contemporary Spanish conductor from a city just north of Madrid. His arrangements feature such traditional Spanish instruments as tambourine and castanets. It has also been adapted for the guitar — perhaps the most Spanish instrument of all.

Andalusian music is the kind of Spanish music we most frequently hear, so let us start our survey of six of the eight movements which go to make up Albéniz's *Suite Española* with the music of Seville, the capital of Andalusia.

Instruments of Spain

1. The **guitar** is a plucked stringed instrument with a fretted finger board, i.e. with bars across the finger board marking off the positions of different notes.

2. The **zanfoña** is a mechanically bowed stringed instrument of Galicia and the Asturias.

3. The **zampoña** is a term used in some parts of Spain to refer to a kind of bagpipe.

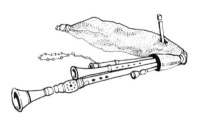

4. The **fluviol** is a small pipe of the Pyrenees, often played one-handed together with a small drum.

GUIDE TO THE MUSIC

Sevilla (Seville)

The dance-music of this town is known as the *Sevillanas*. The lively introduction uses the pulsing rhythm ♪♪♪ ♪ ♪♪ to set the mood for the melody which follows.

Contrasting with the opening vivacity, there soon occurs a widely-scored flexible melody which seems to paint the shimmer of the midday sun beating down on the dusty streets of Seville.

The music builds up in intensity to a repeat of the opening melody.

Cataluña (Catalonia)

The dance of the Cataluña district is a *Corranda* or running dance. In $\frac{6}{8}$ time, it has an aggressive severity which is quite different from the *Sevillanas*.

If you look carefully at the music, you will see that the note below G varies between F sharp and F natural. An eight-note scale including F natural and F sharp is characteristic of some Spanish music. The **zanfoña** (a kind of Spanish hurdy-gurdy) was tuned to this scale.

Granada

This *Serenata* (Serenade) is typical of the music which you might well hear on a visit to Granada as a romantic señor serenades his señorita to the accompaniment of a strumming guitar.

The Alhambra Palace, Granada

The music is quietly amorous and the triplet figure ( ) is a 'fingerprint' of the tune, a motif also found in *Sevillanas* which we have already heard.

The music takes on a sadder, more reflective quality with this plaintive phrase.

Then the charming smoothness of the opening tune returns. Again the serenader becomes sad and reflective, and only at the end of the piece does he find comfort in the opening melody.

Asturias

The *Leyenda* (the dance of this part of Spain) has the sound of what most people would consider to be the typical flamenco music for guitar: rapidly-repeated notes and a melody twining round them.

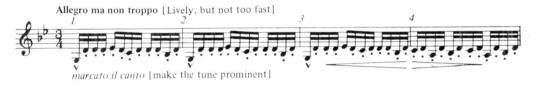

After this texture has built up to a tremendous climax and died away, you hear the same kind of bare octave melodies which the composer used in *Sevillanas*.

After a tentative return to the opening guitar-type music the piece moves forward to an even bigger climax, and after a short reference to the middle section it ends quietly.

A serenade — 1880s style

Cadiz

For the most part these pieces depict the music of the places named in their titles rather than their physical appearance and atmosphere. But in the *Canción* of Cadiz the atmosphere of the music suggests this town on a sunny, warm day. The triplet 'fingerprint' is present in the rhythm of the lower parts throughout much of this movement ( ), and the smooth, flowing tune above pictures the whitewashed houses of Cadiz ranged beside the blue sea.

Again listen out for the wide-spaced bare octave melodies which you should easily recognise towards the end of the piece.

Castilla (Castile)

The *Seguidillas*, danced in Castilla, is a very lively dance and the opening of Albéniz's piece suggests the strumming of the guitar.

A tune in bare octaves, widely-scored (you should now be very familiar with this sound), interrupts the flow of the music on several occasions, but after each interruption the strumming of the guitar returns.

This phrase is extended later in the piece to make an animated tune, but the strumming guitar idea is never far away, and in a flourish it brings the piece to a brilliant close.

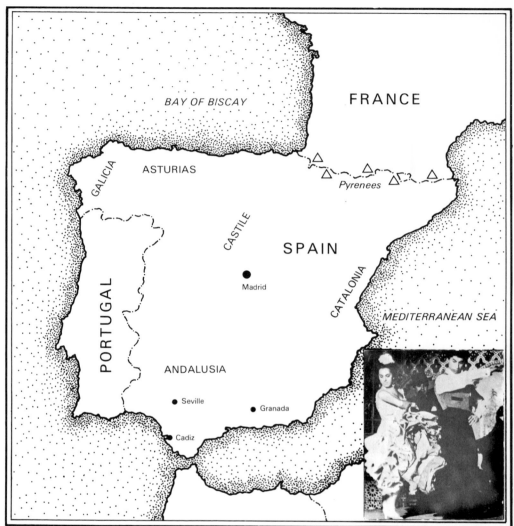

➡ *FOLLOW UP*

1. Find out what you can about Spanish *flamenco* dance, its music, dance steps and traditional costume. Make wall pictures with maps, drawings and photographs to illustrate what you have found out about Spanish folk music. The information here will give you a start.

2. Listen to 'Seguidilla' from Act 1 of Bizet's opera *Carmen* and discuss to what extent you think this music is similar to Albéniz's musical portrait of Castile.

Sinfonia Antartica

BY RALPH VAUGHAN WILLIAMS (1872-1958)

Vaughan Williams was born in the small village of Down Ampney in Gloucestershire. In his twenties he was very interested in collecting English folk songs (much in the same was as Kodály and Bartók did in Hungary). This had a great influence on his musical style, most obviously in his *Fantasia on Greensleeves* and *Folk Song Suite*. He composed nine symphonies, miscellaneous orchestral pieces, two concertos, various operas and vocal pieces and a lot of music for films.

Vaughan Williams tells us in a programme note to his *Sinfonia Antartica* that the work was inspired by the film *Scott of the Antarctic* (1948) for which he wrote the incidental music. Some of the themes are derived from his music to that film, and the symphony was first performed in Manchester in 1953.

Vaughan Williams saw Scott's tragic journey as symbolic of mankind battling against the elements; but although his film score *can* be interpreted at this deeper level there is no doubt that he also intended it to be pictorial, evoking in the music the bleak and menacing Antarctic landscape.

BRITISH ANTARCTIC EXPEDITION, 1910-1913

Robert Falcon Scott (1868-1912), British naval officer and polar explorer, was leader of the British Antarctic Expedition which sailed from Cardiff docks in June 1910 for Ross Island, by way of Australia and New Zealand, with a full scientific programme and with the South Pole as its declared objective.

On arrival at Melbourne, Scott received a telegram which cast gloom across the entire venture. It was from the Norwegian explorer, Roald Amundsen, and read:

'BEG LEAVE TO INFORM YOU
PROCEEDING ANTARCTICA
AMUNDSEN'

The Norwegian explorer was determined to be first to reach the South Pole. His telegram revealed a sudden change of plan. Although his original intention had been to co-operate with Scott on a scientific venture, the expedition had degenerated into a race.

Amundsen, determined to reach the Pole, abandoned all scientific research and made all possible use of his dog-teams. Scott, on the other hand, decided not to abandon his scientific programme entirely; also, he had less faith in dogs and chose to rely on man-power for the last stage of the journey to the Pole. Very bad weather conditions, a delayed start, shortage of food and fuel — all led to disaster. Scott's party of five (Lieutenant Harry Bowers, Captain Lawrence Oates, Dr Edward Wilson, Petty Officer Edgar Evans and Scott himself) finally reached the South Pole on 18 January 1912 only to discover that Amundsen had beaten them to it by four weeks.

Wilson, Scott, Oates, and (seated) Bowers and Evans at the South Pole

THE RETURN JOURNEY

Scott's return journey from the South Pole was even more disastrous. Weather conditions worsened. Food was in short supply. Oates and Evans were suffering from frostbite, Wilson from snow blindness. Evans then had a bad fall in which he sustained severe head injuries; on 17 February he died. Continuing their nightmarish journey, the four remaining members of the party were often unable to cover more than four miles a day.

Oates was now in great pain since his feet were badly frostbitten. In temperatures reaching –37 deg. he bravely attempted to keep pace with his companions, but inevitably his condition was delaying the progress of the journey. About 120 miles from base the party camped and awoke the following morning to find a blizzard raging. While the others remained in their sleeping bags waiting for the blizzard to stop,

Oates walking to his death

Oates with much difficulty got to his feet and said, 'I'm just going outside, and may be some time.' He walked out into the blizzard to his death. So that his companions would not be delayed in their desperate bid for safety, Oates willingly sacrificed his life. Scott records:

It was the act of a brave man and an English gentleman. We all hope to meet the end with a similar spirit, and assuredly the end is not far.

Scott, Wilson, and Bowers struggled on. Hopes were raised when, on 20 March, they set up camp for the night only 11 miles from 'One Ton Depot', where food and fuel were plentiful, and one short march from safety. But the next morning they awoke to a howling blizzard. It raged for nine days. They were trapped without food or fuel.

The last entry in Scott's diary, dated 29 March, reads:

we shall stick it out to the end but we are getting weaker of course and the end cannot be far. It seems a pity but I do not think I can write more —

R Scott

Last Entry
For God's sake look after our people

The bodies of the three explorers, together with Scott's diary, were found eight months later by a search party.

GUIDE TO THE MUSIC

FIRST MOVEMENT

Prelude *Andante maestoso* (Slow and majestically)

The Prelude, which includes the title-music of the film, is headed by a quotation from the poem *Prometheus Unbound* by the English poet Shelley which ends:

To suffer woes which hope thinks infinite,
To forgive wrongs darker than death or night,
To defy power which seems omnipotent,
Neither to change, nor falter, nor repent:
This . . . is to be . . .
Good, great and joyous, beautiful and free,
This is alone life, joy, empire and victory.

This movement is organised in three sections, each representing three different ideas. The opening subject starts as follows:

This theme is used as a whole or in part throughout the work. A few Antarctic shimmerings form a prelude to a soprano solo without words, accompanied by a chorus of sopranos and altos.

The Antarctic landscape is shown first as a white wilderness in the scoring for female chorus and wind machine, then as ice by the cold sounds of the piano, glockenspiel, celesta, and vibraphone.

This is followed by other themes of minor importance which lead up to a theme accompanied by deep bells, which was supposed in the film to be 'menacing'. It also is used frequently throughout the work.

Then, after a repetition of the soprano solo, a trumpet flourish

introduces the coda which is built up largely on the opening theme.

SECOND MOVEMENT

Scherzo *Moderato — poco animando*
(At a moderate pace — becoming livelier)

> *There go the ships*
> *and there is that Leviathan*
> *whom thou hast made to take his*
> *pastime therein.*
>
> from PSALM 104

The second movement is described as a Scherzo (light-hearted, humorous piece) and is descriptive of various episodes in the film.

The Terra Nova and a view from a cavern in a stranded iceberg (1911)

The opening theme is as follows:

This motif for horns represents the deck of Scott's ship, the *Terra Nova*, as it battles its way through the gigantic seas of the Antarctic regions.

This is followed by another little wisp of theme:

Then comes a motif which, if people are looking for a pictorial element in the music, could be taken as representing whales.

The next section could be called the 'trio'. Its tune was used in the film to suggest penguins.

The 'scherzo' music is not repeated, only its rhythm.

The music ends on an indefinite chord for muted brass and celesta.

THIRD MOVEMENT

Landscape *Lento* (Very slow)

> *Ye ice falls! Ye that from the mountain's brow*
> *Adown enormous ravines slope amain —*

The music here is chiefly atmospheric but the following themes may be noted:

'Landscape' is a tone-picture of the Antarctic and such brief themes as there are scored using a wide range of colours in the orchestra. The instruments used in 'Landscape' are:

soprano solo	3 flutes (3rd doubling piccolo)	timpani
small chorus	2 oboes	percussion (3 or 4 players):
	1 cor anglais	triangle
strings	2 clarinets	cymbals
	1 bass clarinet	side drum
harp	2 bassoons	bass drum
celesta	1 double bassoon	gong
pianoforte		bells
organ	4 horns	glockenspiel
	3 trumpets	xylophone
	3 trombones	vibraphone
	1 tuba	wind machine

You can see pictures of some of these instruments on the next page.

27

Some percussion instruments

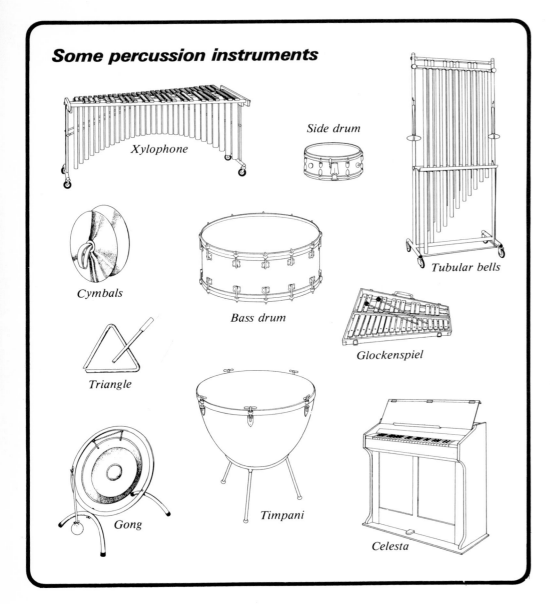

Xylophone

Side drum

Tubular bells

Cymbals

Bass drum

Glockenspiel

Triangle

Gong

Timpani

Celesta

Out of this music (concerned mainly with sounds and combinations of instruments) suddenly emerge some chords played on the full organ. The effect of this is shattering. Vaughan Williams is attempting to portray the 'ice falls' of the poem by Samuel Taylor Coleridge which heads this movement. The music leads without a break to the fourth movement.

FOURTH MOVEMENT

Intermezzo   *Andante sostenuto* (Slow and sustained)

> *Love, all alike, no season knows, or clime,*
> *Nor hours, days, months, which are the rags of time*
>   from THE SUN RISING (John Donne)

The movement that follows is a relief from the inhumanity of Nature. In the film there is a reference to Scott's wife, and the quotation from John Donne's poem *The Sun Rising* suggests that human affection still has some part to play in man's battle against the forces of Nature.   There are two main themes:

Towards the end of the movement the bell passage reappears, followed by some very soft music connected in the film with the death of Oates.

FIFTH MOVEMENT

Epilogue   *Alla marcia moderato* (In moderate march tempo)

The 'Epilogue' starts with another flourish.

Then follows a march tune, obviously suggested by the opening of the 'Prelude'.

Other themes follow leading to a big climax. (In the film this passage accompanies the blizzard which finally defeated Scott.) The bell passage comes in again, suddenly very soft. The voices are heard again and the opening flourish, first loud and then soft, leads to a complete repetition of the beginning of the 'Prelude'.

Voices and wind machine alternate with a solo soprano voice who sings a forlorn lament.

The grave of Captain Scott, Dr. Wilson, and Lieutenant Bowers

I do not regret this journey; we took risks, we knew we took them, things have come out against us, therefore we have no cause for complaint.

from CAPTAIN SCOTT'S JOURNAL

⟹ FOLLOW UP

Imagine yourself as the music co-ordinator for a film studio. Using the music you have got to know well in *Portraits in Music* say what kind of film (or episode in a film) you think each piece would be suitable for as soundtrack/background music. Consider as wide a variety of film types and documentaries as possible in your selection.

Film music

'I believe that film music is a fine art, but it is applied art, and a specialised art at that.'

Ralph Vaughan Williams's comments in *The Royal College of Music Magazine* (1944) make the point that the musician composing film music must be prepared to write music which both follows the form of the drama and is capable of almost unlimited extension or compression; it must be able to 'fade-out' or 'fade-in' again without loss of continuity.

Music in films fulfils many different functions. The composer of a film score must take into account what actually appears on the screen (and for how long) and match his music accordingly. In diagram form he might think of it like this:

Time factor (In seconds)	0	5	10
1. ACTION ON FILM:			
2. DIALOGUE:			
3. SOUND TRACK EFFECTS (other than dialogue):			
4. MUSIC:			

and his music must co-ordinate appropriately with the first three elements.

Problems with which he may have to deal and accommodate in the music score include: sudden change of scene/mood, generating emotional tension/relaxation, appropriate characterisation (music for the hero, heroine, villain of the piece, etc.).

The sound track, including music, is recorded on the side of the celluloid film in a continuous strip which is fed through the projector.

The Execution of Stepan Razin

CHORAL AND ORCHESTRAL PIECE

BY DMITRI SHOSTAKOVICH (1906-1975)

Shostakovich was born in St. Petersburg (now Leningrad). He composed symphonies, operas, instrumental pieces and film music, and many of these works were inspired by communist ideals. He was, however, not always in sympathy with the politics of the ruling communist government. In 1936 one of his compositions failed to please Stalin, and he fell into political disfavour, but this eclipse was only temporary.

Stepan Razin was the leader of a rebellion of brigands and peasants on Russia's south-eastern frontier between 1667 and 1671. In the first three years of his campaign he carried out daring raids on Russian and Persian villages. In 1670, he decided to lead his force of 7,000 Cossacks (old name for the people of S.E. Russia) in revolt against the Tsar of Russia. He attacked the fortress-cities on the banks of the Volga, capturing Tsaritsyn (Volgograd) and Astrakhan, and in the victory celebrations the conquerers revelled in drunken orgies and committed appalling atrocities.

Military success together with growing support from peasants and town workers encouraged Razin to continue his advance northwards. Wherever he went he added to his numbers (by this time around 20,000).

The Tsar was alarmed by the extent of Razin's success, so he sent a large and well-equipped army to combat his forces, which were now outside the walls of Simbirsk (Ulyanovsk). In October 1670 a confrontation took place there between the Tsar's army and Razin's forces. The well-trained soldiers were more than a match for Razin's undisciplined followers, who were decisively defeated. Razin fled from the battlefield, but was finally captured in April 1671 and taken to Moscow; there he was tortured, and publicly executed in June of that year. His death brought an end to the rebellion.

Razin's forces were made up of two groups: peasants inspired by hatred of legalised slavery and brigands bent on plunder and destruction. Russian historians have tended to concentrate on his acts of aggression, while his fight for social justice has been neglected. However, in the folklore of Russia, Razin is a revolutionary hero; his adventures have caught the imagination of many Russian artists, writers, and composers.

The 20th-century Russian poet, Yevgeny Yevtushenko, has written a highly dramatic and emotional poem on the death of Stepan Razin which Dmitri Shostakovich, a leading Soviet composer, set to music. *The Execution of Stepan Razin* is written for bass solo, chorus, and orchestra.

A Cossack warrior on horseback

Stepan Razin's head by the Soviet painter Surikov (1848-1916) (from the Russian Museum of Art, Leningrad)

GUIDE TO THE MUSIC

1. The composer uses an orchestral introduction, with harsh chords from the brass section presented in savage rhythmic patterns, to set a highly-charged mood of drama.

2. A **soloist** and **male chorus** set the scene in a series of short episodes: the mob assembles; the Tsar prepares himself to appear in the streets; people are in a holiday mood; merchants sell their wares; jesters entertain in the square; old men shuffle by. To create the effect of mounting excitement in his music Shostakovich

(a) punctuates the narrative with male chorus interruptions 'They're bringing Stenka Razin', which come more and more frequently as Stepan approaches (Stenka is the familiar term for Stepan);

Listen for: *'Sten'ku Razina vezut!'* ('They're bringing Stenka Razin')

(b) has the orchestra take up the excited comment of the chorus after each outburst;
(c) provides a different orchestral accompaniment for the picture presented in each verse by the soloist. The triangle used in the third picture suggest the clowning antics of a nobleman's son.

3. Some drunken women hurry by. Here Shostakovich introduces a new 'colour' — a **female chorus**, accompanied by tambourine — just at the point when we are beginning to tire of the soloist and male chorus.

4. To the accompaniment of screams, and spat upon from all sides, Razin, dressed in a white shirt, appears in an open cart. The cry 'They're bringing Stenka Razin' comes for the last time.

Listen for: *'Sten'ku Razina vezut!'*

Shostakovich brings the music to a climax through the combination of both male and female voices. Listen for the extraordinary shrieks of the chorus (Ai! Oi! Eeh!) expressed in octave *glissandi* (sliding over the notes between one pitch and another) and the wild sounds of the full orchestra.

5. Razin stands silent before the crowd and smiles bitterly to himself. The crowd spits on him.

Listen for: *'plyuitye, plyuitye, plyuitye'* ('spit, spit, spit')

Detached chords from lower woodwind and plucked strings suggest the revulsion of the crowd as they spit. Razin reflects on the situation in which he finds himself, but the chorus breaks up his thoughts. They see him as an enemy, an outlaw and a revolutionary against the ruling classes.

6. Razin reflects on his torture: his captors beat him on the mouth with rope. Brutal brass chords suggest the blows of the rope. He doesn't give way and spitting blood, cries:

A rebel against the boyars (aristocrats)? — true.
A rebel against the people? — no.

**Listen for the chorus repeating his words:**
'Suprotiv boyarstva — pravda
Suprotiv naroda — nyet.'

7. Razin doesn't think he has done wrong in hanging aristocrats from turrets. In his own eyes he is only guilty of hanging too few of them. The music changes its mood at this point, perhaps in keeping with the new tone expressed in the words. He has committed murder in his fight for a 'good' Tsar, but is now disillusioned about what this really means.

A short orchestral interlude suggests Razin's approach to the block, and tubular bells are used in the orchestra to suggest the bells of the city.

8. The executioner's leather apron flaps in the breeze and in his hands he holds aloft the blue axe, blue as the Volga. As Razin stands before the executioner the sight of the axe reminds him of the blue river, and in a dream-like state he imagines boats sailing along its silvery surface. At this point the music has a timeless quality — the action is suspended, as often happens in a moment of fear.

Stepan Razin's execution

9. Before he places his head on the block, Razin takes a last look around him and senses that the crowd are beginning to be aware of the oppression of the aristocracy and share his revolutionary spirit. Reassured, he feels he has not lived in vain, and with his chin resting on the jagged edge of the block asks for the axe.

Listen for: *'Davai, topor'* ('Give me the axe')

10. Off rolls his head, aflame with blood, and it mutters: 'Not in vain . . .'

Listen for: *'Nye zazrya . . .'* ('Not in vain')

To emphasise Stepan's triumph, Shostakovich sets the words muttered by the dismembered corpse to bold music and the words are repeated over and over. The death-like silence that settles over Execution Place is interrupted by officers who ask the people why they are not celebrating the death of Stepan Razin.

11. At this point woodwind, accompanied by tambourine, play a tune for dancing, but the merriment is short-lived and there is a return to the silence — only the sound of fleas jumping (listen for the xylophone) from poor to rich is audible. The hushed crowd remove their hats and the great bells of Moscow are again heard.

12. But heavy with blood the head moves; it turns from Execution Place towards where the poor live and its glances are full of accusation. The mood of revolution is matched by menacing music.

13. A priest comes forward to close the eyelids of the severed head, but with a supernatural force the pupils of the eyes push away his hands. The head mockingly begins to laugh at the Tsar. The following music introduces this sinister episode.

Su - ye - tyas', dro - zha - shchiy po - pik pod - lye - tyel. Vye - ki Sten' - ki - ny za - kryt' on Kho - tyel.

14. The piece ends with a picture of the defiant Stepan, triumphant over the Tsar — even in death.

Map of S.E. Russia showing the towns captured by Stepan Razin

View of the river Volga

☞ *FOLLOW UP*

1. Tell the story of *Stepan Razin* in your own words and, if you like, draw a picture to illustrate your story.

2. Look in the *Radio Times* (radio and television sections) and see how many pieces by Russian composers are being broadcast. Make a list and compare results with your friends. See if any of the pieces or composers mentioned on page 36 are featured.

ROMEO AND JULIET

FANTASY OVERTURE

BY PETER ILICH TCHAIKOVSKY (1840-1893)

Tchaikovsky began his working life as a civil servant, but at 23 abandoned his chosen career to study music at the conservatory of St. Petersburg. His character was a curious mixture of sensitiveness and excitability, qualities which are clearly expressed in his *Romeo and Juliet* overture. His life included some strange events: he separated from his wife after only eleven weeks of marriage, and he entered into an unusual relationship with a wealthy widow, Nadezhda von Meck, whom he never actually met but with whom he corresponded for years; her financial support allowed Tchaikovsky to devote himself to composition. He died from cholera after unwisely drinking unboiled water despite warnings from friends.

Romeo and Juliet is a tragedy by Shakespeare about a family feud. The Montagues and Capulets, two families in the Italian town of Verona, are literally at daggers drawn, and duelling in the streets between members of the two families is a common occurrence.

Romeo (a Montague) falls in love with Juliet (a Capulet). Because their families would never allow such a match they can meet only under cover of darkness; Romeo comes to the Capulets' garden and talks to Juliet, who comes out on to the balcony of her bedroom. They arrange to be married secretly by Friar Laurence, who sympathises with their unfortunate situation. Unluckily Romeo, drawn into a street duel against his will, kills Juliet's cousin Tybalt in self-defence and is forced to leave Verona immediately after the marriage to escape the forces of the law. Friar Laurence arranges a complicated plot to bring the lovers together again, but everything goes wrong. Romeo, thinking Juliet is dead, takes poison. When she realises her husband is poisoned, Juliet joins Romeo in death by stabbing herself.

Tchaikovsky composed his 'Fantasy Overture' based on this subject in 1870.

GUIDE TO THE MUSIC

1. The piece opens with a motif which is reminiscent of a Russian hymn-tune.

The sombre orchestral colouring of the low clarinet suggests the tragic background to the story, and perhaps represents the religious spirit of Friar Laurence.

2. The mood brightens when flute, clarinet and harp rise from the low register.

3. After this slow introduction the first theme of the main quick section takes on a highly energetic character.

Duelling Theme A

The strong, syncopated (off-the-beat) rhythm expresses Romeo's defiant temperament. It is easy to picture the cut and thrust of the swords in this music.

Duelling Theme B

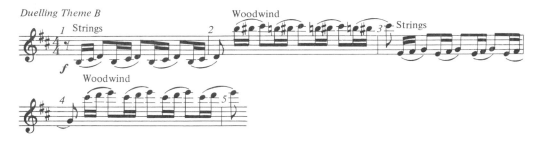

These rolling figures in the strings, with sharp exchanges from the woodwinds, drive forward to a climax which is reached with the repetition of Duelling Theme **A** in the full orchestra.

4. After this climax in the duelling music, the tension gradually subsides into the romance of the meeting between Romeo and Juliet in the balcony scene. Cor anglais and violas give out this plaintive melody:

Romance Theme

Muted strings add an epilogue; this quiet passage seems to suggest the warm summer night in the garden. Both motifs are repeated — the Romance Theme is increased in intensity by flute and oboe, while the epilogue is taken up by the harp.

5. But soon the duelling music returns and through it we hear Friar Laurence working to bring together the young people in love. The Friar Laurence Theme in the French horns is combined with that of the two Duelling Themes.

Romeo and Juliet — still from the film by Franco Zeffirelli with Leonard Whiting as Romeo and Olivia Hussey as Juliet

The cor anglais

Oboe

Cor anglais

The name means 'English horn' but it is neither English nor a horn. It is a member of the oboe family, but pitched slightly lower than the oboe. Notice that its reed is bent backwards. Its bell is pear-shaped, ends in a small opening, a feature of its design which accounts for its soft, somewhat melancholy tone quality. This is probably why Tchaikovsky chose it to convey the fated relationship of Romeo and Juliet. Other examples of its use occur in the slow movement of Dvorak's *New World Symphony* and in the orchestral accompaniment to the 'Flower Song' in Bizet's opera *Carmen*.

6. The climax is reached when the Friar Laurence Theme is taken over by two trumpets, while the full orchestra accompanies with the syncopated rhythms of Duelling Theme **A**.

7. The duelling music rises to a new intensity, and when next the love-music is heard there is an undercurrent of restlessness and an air of tragedy as Romeo is telling Juliet that he has killed her cousin, and must escape from Verona. The intensity of the Romance Theme is increased in its scoring for violins and flutes, and culminates in a final quotation of Duelling Theme **A**.

8. A slow, quiet concluding section is built on a sadly reflective version of the Romance Theme. The ominous drum taps and this transformation of the love-music foreshadow the tragic end of Romeo and Juliet.

Another scene from the film:
Tybalt lies dead while Juliet's mother and the prince of Verona look on in horror

Russian composers and their music

Instrumental and vocal music in Russia in the 19th century was dominated by the spirit of folk music. The first composer to use the distinctive melodic and rhythmic features of Russian folk song was Glinka (1804-1857). He was popularly known as 'the father of Russian music'. In his opera *Russlan and Ludmilla* Glinka also introduced colourful effects derived from the music of oriental Russia.

Tchaikovsky, besides composing *Romeo and Juliet* and other similar symphonic fantasies, was the first great Russian symphonist; the last of his six symphonies (*Pathétique*, 1893) is perhaps the best known. The tradition of Tchaikovsky's concerto writing was continued by Rachmaninoff, whose Piano Concerto No. 2 is widely performed. The melancholy mood of much of Tchaikovsky's music contrasts vividly with the vigorous national style of Borodin, 1833-1887, (*Polovstian Dances*), Mussorgsky, 1839-1881, (*Pictures at an Exhibition*), and Rimsky-Korsakov, 1844-1908, (*Scheherezade*).

In the 20th century Russia has produced highly regarded composers in Stravinsky, 1882-1975, Prokofiev, 1891-1953, and Shostakovich, 1906-1975. (See pages 30-33.)

Prokofiev

Delius

Leonard Bernstein

▭➡ *FOLLOW UP*

1. Franz Liszt, the famous Hungarian composer and piano virtuoso, saw the music of the 19th century as entering a new phase in illustrating definite subjects. To what extent do you think that Tchaikovsky illustrates the drama of the Romeo and Juliet story in his music?

2. The Romeo and Juliet theme has been treated since Tchaikovsky's day by a number of composers, notably Serge Prokofiev in his ballet *Romeo and Juliet*, Leonard Bernstein in his musical *West Side Story* (subsequently turned into an Oscar-winning film) and Frederick Delius in his opera *A Village Romeo and Juliet*. Find out what you can about any one of these pieces.

Academic Festival Overture

BY JOHANNES BRAHMS (1833-1897)

Brahms was born in Hamburg, the son of a musician who played the double bass in the theatres of the city. While undergoing a thorough musical training by day Brahms supported himself by playing the piano in cafes and dance halls by night. He was encouraged to continue his attempts at composition by the composers Franz Liszt and Robert Schumann. For four years Brahms held a position at the German court, moved to Switzerland for a year or two, and finally settled in Vienna where he spent the last 35 years of his life. His daily routine became something of a ritual, beginning at 5 a.m. with the brewing of strong coffee and the smoking of an equally strong cigar, followed by many others during the course of the day.

In March 1879 Breslau University honoured Brahms by conferring on him the degree of Doctor of Philosophy in recognition of his services to German music. As a token of his gratitude he composed an overture for the University and called it 'Overture for an academic festival.' Although Brahms never actually attended a university he was no stranger to student life. In 1853, when the sketch on this page was done, he joined in student revels at Göttingen where his friend the great violinist

Joachim was attending lectures, and the two of them were involved in playing a trick on a new student round the common room table of the students' club. At the first performance of the overture on 4 January 1881 Brahms described it as:

GUIDE TO THE MUSIC

1. The overture opens quietly.

2. A more sustained tune on the violas, then taken up by the horns, follows.

3. A return to the opening mood is interrupted by a sudden outburst from the full orchestra.

4. Like the sun rising on a new day, trumpets give out the first of the student songs Brahms uses in his overture.

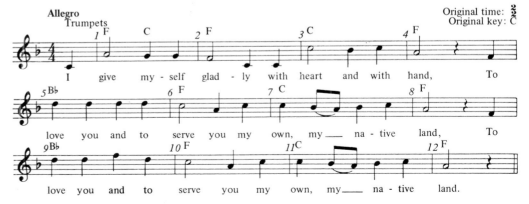

37

5. Soon a new theme is announced by strings

6. and is followed by a modified version of the second student song.

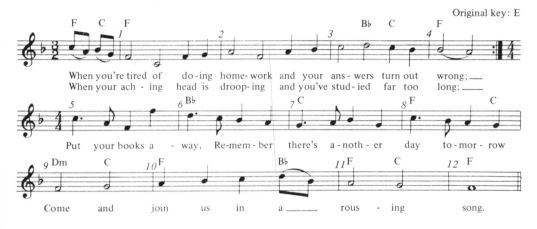

When you're tired of do-ing home-work and your ans-wers turn out wrong;—
When your ach-ing head is droop-ing and you've stud-ied far too long;—

Put your books a - way, Re-mem-ber there's a-noth-er day to-mor-row

Come and join us in a ____ rous - ing song.

Göttingen, where Brahms joined in student revels. Photograph taken in 1859.

The bassoon

Brahms features the bassoon in his scoring of the 'Fox's Song'. It is the bass of the woodwind section in the orchestra, and owing to the length of its tube it is bent back on itself. It is made in five sections. When in pieces it is like a bundle of firewood (hence the Italian term for it is *fagotto*!). The instrument is even in tone colour throughout its range, although the lowest notes tend to be rather thick and reedy. Sometimes known as the clown of the orchestra (its role in the 'Fox's Song'?) it can also play all kinds of expressive music and blends well with French horns.

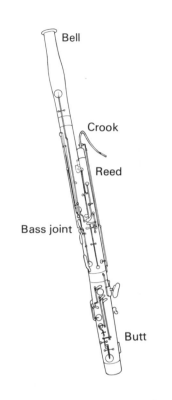

range:

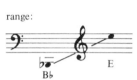

7. This leads almost immediately into the third of the student songs, the 'Fox's Song' (new students were called 'foxes').

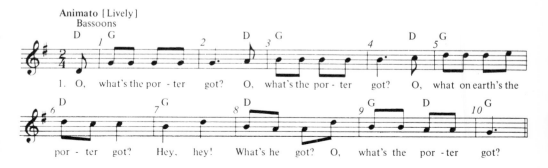

1. O, what's the por - ter got? O, what's the por - ter got? O, what on earth's the

por - ter got? Hey, hey! What's he got? O, what's the por - ter got?

8. The overture continues with references to tunes you have already heard, and the final playing of the 'Fox's Song' climaxes in a majestic 'coda', or conclusion, which introduces for the first time the well-known student song '*Gaudeamus igitur*' played mainly by brass instruments against a background of swirling string passages.

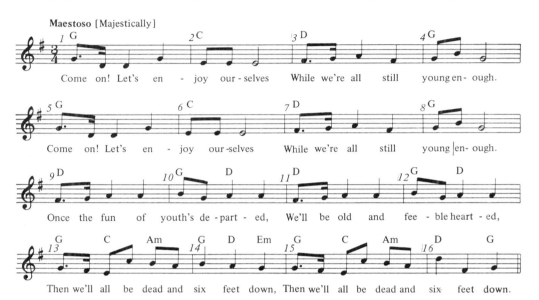

Come on! Let's en - joy our-selves While we're all still young en- ough.

Come on! Let's en - joy our -selves While we're all still young en- ough.

Once the fun of youth's de - part - ed, We'll be old and fee - ble heart - ed,

Then we'll all be dead and six feet down, Then we'll all be dead and six feet down.

⮕ *FOLLOW UP*

1. Once you are thoroughly familiar with the themes of this overture, listen very carefully again to the pieces and list the themes (or parts of themes) as they occur. If you manage to spot something like 20 references you will have done very well indeed.

2. Learn to sing the four student songs quoted — with guitar accompaniment, if possible.

Vienna in the time of Brahms

Students at Göttingen University exchanging greetings

ENIGMA VARIATIONS

BY EDWARD ELGAR (1857-1934)

Born at Broadheath near Worcester, Elgar was the son of an organist and music seller. As a youngster he learned to play piano, violin, 'cello, double bass, bassoon and trombone, and took part in local music making playing whichever instrument was required. From 21-27 he was the bandmaster of the staff in a lunatic asylum, which gave him his first experience in conducting. As a composer he was largely self-taught and it was a long time before he rose to the front rank of British composers. His *Enigma Variations* (written when Elgar was 42) assured him of this position. In 1904 he was knighted and 20 years later he became Master of the King's Musick, official recognition of his contribution to the music of Edwardian England. (On page 45 you can see a note from Elgar to the Lord Chamberlain of the time. It shows just how little the composer's early musical training cost.)

Air and variations

Air and Variations is one of the oldest forms in music. There are three basic elements which go to make up musical style: melody, rhythm, and timbre (tone quality). Composers may alter all these elements of the 'air' or main theme in the 'variations'.

The 'Enigma' Variations were written at Malvern in 1899. The piece opens with the 'Enigma' theme (the melody and its accompaniment), followed by 14 variations. As a title each variation bears a set of initials, a name, or some other sign; these identify friends of Elgar and the variations are musical sketches of these friends. (The first variation is a portrait of Elgar's wife; the finale is a self-portrait.) The entire piece is dedicated to 'My friends pictured within'.

The word 'enigma' means 'puzzle'. Elgar was fascinated by puzzles. He let it be known that the 'Enigma' theme, which appears in most of the variations was in fact a counter-melody to another well-known theme — in other words, the two themes could be played together.

But, as you will notice once you have listened to the whole piece, the other theme is not played in Elgar's variations. Elgar provided only a few unhelpful clues for the many people who have since tried to identify this well-known theme. Suggested 'solutions' include 'God save the King', 'Auld Lang Syne', even 'Pop goes the weasel'. Another suggestion is that it was all a joke and the theme is not a counter-melody to anything at all!

As you follow the opening of Elgar's theme, notice the sad, yearning quality of the music. You will see, from looking at the first six bars of the music, how Elgar makes his tune climb towards a high point (in fact, the highest note of the melody is in bar 3), before descending towards bar 6. The effect is of increasing emotional intensity, dying down again to a point of repose. If you look carefully at these six opening bars you will see that there is a one-pulse rest at the beginning of each; this makes the music sound somewhat hesitant. In bar 7 the music changes to a contrasting, brighter mood, with a continuous line of melody played by the warm-toned clarinets and other woodwind instruments. The music of the opening section returns (played, as before, on violins), and the theme ends peacefully.

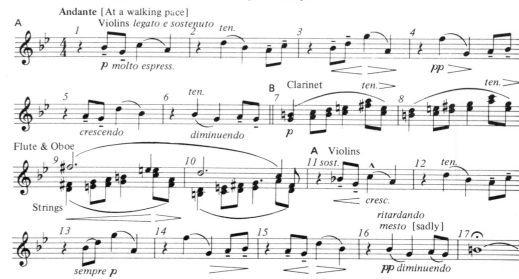

GUIDE TO THE MUSIC

I C.A.E.

Caroline Alice Elgar — the composer's wife. The tune Elgar used to whistle to tell his wife he was home is printed in small notes in the example below. The theme leads straight into the first variation, which is really an extension of it with, as Elgar said, 'romantic and delicate additions'. His wife was a constant source of inspiration to him.

II H.D.S-P.

Hew David Steuart-Powell, a well-known amateur pianist who played chamber music with B.G.N. (cello — see Variation XII) and Elgar (violin) for many years. His characteristic run over the keys before beginning to play is here humorously suggested by the semiquaver passages.

III R.B.T.

Richard Baxter Townshend, a scholar and eccentric. His precise manner of speaking is expressed in the opening oboe melody (described by Elgar as a 'somewhat pert' version of the theme), and his grumpiness is portrayed by bassoons at the end of the variation. The story is told of R.B.T.'s riding a tricycle in Oxford — he would ring the bell continuously to let people know he was coming because, being slightly deaf, he certainly could not hear them!

IV W.M.B.

William Meath Baker, a country squire and scholar, who entertained guests at his country home. In the days of horses and carriages it was difficult to arrange the carriages for a large number of people and Elgar wrote this variation after an occasion when W.M.B. had read out the arrangements for the day and hurriedly left the music-room, banging the door behind him. Bars 15-24 suggest the guests teasing their host.

V R.P.A.

Richard P. Arnold, son of Matthew Arnold, the poet.
He was a great lover of music and played the piano in a
self-taught manner. His conversation, Elgar tells us, was
continually broken up by whimsical and witty remarks.
The theme is solemnly played by the basses, followed by
a light-hearted joking passage on the woodwind.

Moderato [At a moderate pace]

VI YSOBEL

Miss Isabel Fitton — one of Elgar's viola pupils; hence
the viola solos. Perhaps the bassoons' brief comments
on the viola solos represent the relationship of pupil and
teacher in a music lesson. Notice, as Elgar points out,
that the opening bar, a phrase used throughout the
variation, is in fact an ' "exercise" for crossing the
strings — a difficulty for beginners'.

VII TROYTE

Arthur Troyte Griffith, a well-known architect in
Malvern and a forceful personality. The uncouth rhythm
of the drums and lower strings convey the architect's
clumsy attempts to play the piano, and later the strong
rhythm suggests the intervention of the instructor
(Elgar). The final despairing 'slam' probably represents
the banging of the piano lid.

Presto [Fast]

VIII W.N.

Miss Winifred Norbury — a lady of sedate charm, set
here against the background of her 18th century house
among the 'gracious personalities of the ladies' as Elgar
wrote. Oboe trills (from bar 9 onwards) suggest her
light-hearted laughter.

IX NIMROD

Nimrod was Elgar's nickname for his friend A. J. Jaeger, who inspired this variation. (This was a particularly appropriate name since Nimrod is a hunter who appears in the Old Testament, and 'Jaeger' is the German word for 'hunter'.) This variation, like some of the others, is not a complete portrait, Elgar tells us; some represent only a mood, others recall an incident known only to the two people concerned. This one — possibly the most famous in the work — doesn't convey the more fiery aspect of his friend's character. Instead, it is a record of a long summer evening talk, when the two friends discussed the slow movements of Beethoven; the opening bars of this variation are in fact made to sound like the slow movement of a Beethoven piano sonata (the 'Pathétique').

X DORABELLA

Miss Dora Penny, the daughter of friends, whose nickname was Dorabella, a character in the opera 'Così fan tutte' by Mozart. The movement, a delicate, dainty, fluttering portrait suggesting her 'dance like lightness' as Elgar wrote, is headed 'Intermezzo' and is not, strictly speaking, a variation, as it contains no reference to the 'Enigma' theme. The young lady's slight stammer can be heard in the opening, and listen, too, for the inner sustained phrases at first on the viola (bar 10) and later on the flute.

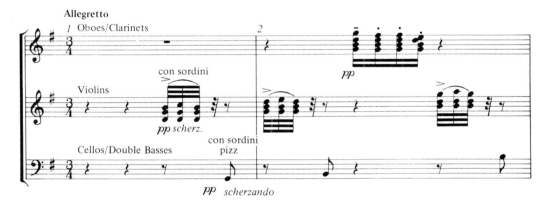

The hills near Malvern

XI G.R.S.

George Robertson Sinclair, the organist of Hereford Cathedral. The variation, however, as Elgar wrote, has nothing to do with organs or cathedrals, nor indeed much with G.R.S. The composer tells us that the first four bars were suggested by the organist's great bulldog Dan '(a well-known character) falling down a steep bank into the river Wye (bar 1); his paddling up-stream to find a landing place (bars 2 and 3); and his rejoicing bark on landing (2nd half of bar 5)'. It was Dr. Sinclair's suggestion to Elgar to set such a scene that inspired this movement.

XII B.G.N.

Basil G. Nevinson, a distinguished amateur cellist who was the third member of the piano trio with H.D.S-P. (piano — see Variation II) and Elgar (violin). He was a close friend of Elgar, who wrote: 'The variation is a tribute to a very dear friend whose scientific and artistic attainments and the whole-hearted way they were put at the disposal of his friends, particularly endeared him to the writer' (i.e. Elgar).

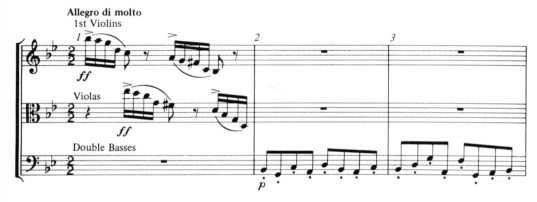

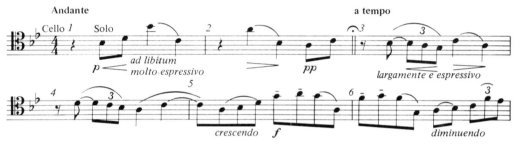

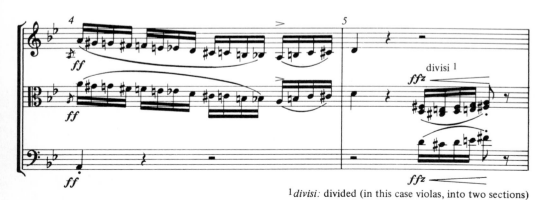

XIII * * *

'The asterisks take the place of the name of a lady' Elgar tells us, 'who was, at the time of composition, on a sea voyage'. Her name was Lady Mary Lygon, a friend of Elgar and his wife. Elgar also writes: 'The drums suggest the distant throb of engines of a liner, over which the clarinet quotes a phrase from Mendelssohn's *Calm Sea and Prosperous Voyage* (an overture).

[1]*divisi:* divided (in this case violas, into two sections)

XIV E.D.U.

Elgar himself, 'Edoo' being his wife's pet name for him. The movement makes a bold and vigorous finale written, as Elgar tells us, in reply to friends who were at the time 'dubious and generally discouraging' as to his musical future. It contains references to Variation I (his wife) and Variation IX (Nimrod), two people who greatly influenced his life and composing. The whole work ends with a triumphant presentation of the Enigma theme in the major key.

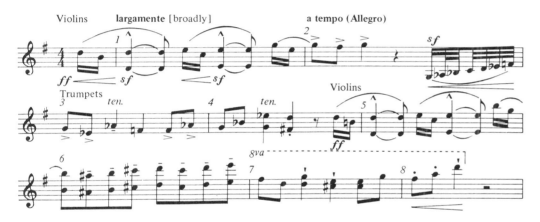

☛ *FOLLOW UP*

1. Once you are thoroughly familiar with the musical portraits of Elgar's *Enigma Variations*, make up a listening quiz to see whether you can identify musical extracts by naming the characters they portray. Take it in turns to start the recording at different points while the rest of the class writes down which variation is being played.

2. Look at the note about the cost of part of Elgar's musical training. Try and work out how much Elgar might have had to pay today for one year's piano and violin lessons, plus books and music.

As Master of the King's Musick Edward Elgar came cheap! Elgar was self-taught, and his musical and general education was costed by the composer himself in an account drawn up in Elgar's own handwriting on note-paper of the Lord Chamberlain's office.

Expenses, *in full,* for general and musical education.	£	s.	d.
1866 School 4 years			
7 Miss Walsh,			
8 11 Britannia Square,			
9 at £1 per qr.	16	0	0
1870 3 years.			
1 Mr Reeve,			
2 Littleton House, Lower Wick,	18	0	0
£1 10s. per qr.			
Books and music Grammar, geography, etc. Pianoforte instruction bk, etc.	2	15	0
Pianoforte lessons, 2 qrs Before 9 yrs old	1	0	0
Violin lessons, Mr Spray, Worcester, 2 qrs 1874	3	0	0
Violin lessons, Mr Politzer, 1877-8	15	15	0
	56	10	0

Elgar's birthplace at Broadheath near Worcester. It is now a museum which contains many interesting exhibits relating to Elgar's life and his music. Try to visit it if you live in the area.

Billy the Kid

ORCHESTRAL SUITE

BY AARON COPLAND (b. 1900)

Born in Brooklyn, New York, in 1900 Aaron Copland went to study music in France but returned to settle in New York about 1926. With the coming of 'the talkies' in the early 1930's, he took up opportunities for composing music for film soundtracks. He also has been a highly successful composer of popular ballets, one of which was *Billy the Kid*. The suite is made up of music from this ballet.

The legend of Billy the Kid

Billy the Kid, probably christened Henry McCarty, was born in New York City. He grew up in Silver City, New Mexico, where his mother owned a local boarding house.

**Billy had a notch in his pistol
    for twenty-one men
Before his young manhood
    had reached its sad end.**

American Ballad

Billy the Kid, now calling himself William Bonney, took an active part in the complex series of gunfights known as the Lincoln County War (1877-79). The affair became so serious that President Hayes was forced to request General Lew Wallace to go to New Mexico as territorial governor to restore order.
    Wallace tried to make a deal with Bonney, but the Kid eventually returned to his old profession of horse thief. Eventually he was captured by Pat Garrett, sheriff of Lincoln County, tried for murder and condemned to death. He made a sensational escape from the sheriff's deputies, but one day was

**Shot down by Pat Garrett,
    Who once was his friend.
The young outlaw's life
    Had now come to its end.**

BILLY THE KID.
$500 REWARD.

I will pay $500 reward to any person or persons who will capture William Bonny, alias The Kid, and deliver him to any sheriff of New Mexico. Satisfactory proofs of identity will be required.

LEW. WALLACE,
Governor of New Mexico.

The citizens of New Mexico thought Governor Wallace's offer of a $500 reward inappropriately small for the capture of such a dangerous killer.

Cowboys and chuck wagon

The legends surrounding Billy the Kid were numerous and fanciful; some people said that he was 31 years old when he died, not 21; he could justly claim only eight notches on his pistol, not the legendary 'thrice seven' that clings to his name; a still more improbable legend is that Pat Garrett did not kill him, but that Billy the Kid escaped a second time and survived to a ripe old age in Mexico.

GUIDE TO THE MUSIC

As you follow the music you will notice that Copland quotes (but never note for note) some authentic cowboy songs in his ballet *Billy the Kid*. You could learn to sing them, and if you play the guitar, some of you might like to accompany.

Section 1: 'The Open Frontier'

The action begins and closes on the open prairie.

Section 2: 'Street Scene and Rodeo'

The central portion of the ballet concerns itself with the significant moments in the life of Billy the Kid. The first scene is a street in a frontier town.

Familiar figures amble by.

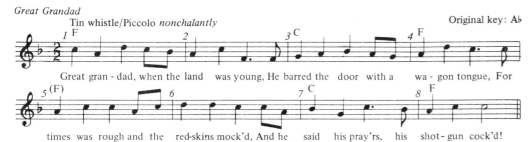

Cowboys saunter into the town, some on horseback, others with lassos.

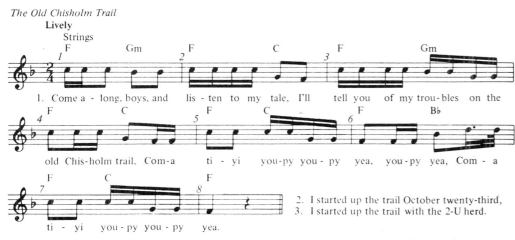

Front Street in the town of Dodge City in the 1880s
Cowboys drinking in a Texas saloon in the 1890s

Some Mexican women do a jarabe (a traditional Mexican dance based on the idea of a man pursuing a girl who continually escapes from him).

Goodbye, Old Paint

Original key: G

1 My foot in the stir-rup, my po-ny won't stand,___ Good-bye, old Paint I'm a-lea-ving Chey-enne. I'm a-lea-ving Chey-enne, I'm off to Mon-ta-na, Good-bye, old Paint, I'm a-lea-ving Chey-enne.

The jarabe is interrupted by a fight between two drunks. Attracted by the gathering crowd, Billy is seen for the first time as a boy of 12 with his mother. The brawl turns ugly, guns are drawn, and somehow Billy's mother is killed. Without hesitation, in cold fury, Billy draws a knife from a cowhand's sheath and stabs his mother's slayers. His short but famous career has begun. In swift succession we see episodes in Billy's later life.

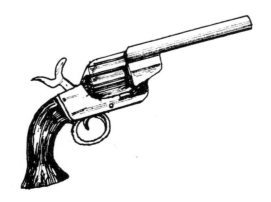

Section 3: 'Card Game'

At night, under the stars, in a quiet card game.

Section 4: 'Billy's Capture'

Hunted by a posse led by his former friend, Pat Garrett, Billy is pursued. A running battle ensues; Billy is captured.

Section 5: 'Dance of Billy's Captors'

A drunken celebration takes place.

Billy in prison is, of course, followed by one of the legendary escapes. Tired and worn out in the desert, Billy rests with his girl. Starting from a deep sleep he sees movements in the shadows. The posse has finally caught up with him.

Riding Free

Rid-ing free. Rid-ing free. There's a price on his head and he's rid-ing free. But the sher-iff with his gun hunts a kill-er on the run and soon he'll shoot him dead. There's a price on Bil-ly's head and soon they'll shoot him dead.

Pat Garrett

Section 6: 'Lament at Billy's Death'

Section 7

There is a return to the music of the opening suggesting the vast expanse of the American prairie lands.

The suite

The idea of collecting together individual pieces of music of contrasting character to form a **suite** began in the 16th and 17th centuries. The suite of this period was usually made up of popular dances. (See Handel's *Water Music* on page 60). In the 19th and 20th centuries, the **orchestral suite**, of which *Billy the Kid* is a typical example, became popular. Composers took music normally heard elsewhere, for example in a theatre, and arranged it for performance in the concert hall. (*Háry János*, by Kodály, is an example of this kind of suite.)

Ballet

A piece of music to accompany dancing on stage. The actions of the characters are danced on stage to the accompaniment of music which pictures the moods of the story. When *Billy the Kid* was performed in the theatre, realistic costumes, scenery and lighting effects helped to give an exciting view of the Wild West.

⌐➔ *FOLLOW UP*

1. Aaron Copland's music for *Billy the Kid* is divided into 6 sections. Divide up a sheet of paper into 6 and as you listen again to the ballet suite draw your own pictures of the 6 sections, beginning a new picture when a new section starts. You will have to work quickly! To help you here is a plan for your page.

1. Open Prairie	2. Street scene	3. Moonlight card game
4. Gunfight and Billy's capture	5. Celebration by Billy's captors	6. Lament at Billy's death

Once you have finished listening to the music perhaps you might like to take time to complete your pictures, or make a mural for your classroom wall telling the story of Billy the Kid's life and death.

2. How does Copland convey the atmosphere of the Wild West in his music?

The 'Varieties' Saloon, Dodge City, Kansas in the 1880s

BILLY THE KID

Billy was a bad man
And carried a big gun,
He was always chasing women
And kept 'em on the run.

He shot men every morning
Just to make a morning meal —
If his gun ran out of bullets
He killed them with cold steel.

He kept his folks in hot water,
And he stole from many a stage,
When his gut was full of liquor
He was always in a rage.

But one day he met a man,
Who was a whole lot badder —
And now he's dead —
And we ain't none the sadder.

Anon. (American Ballad)

PORTSMOUTH POINT

OVERTURE

BY WILLIAM WALTON (b. 1902)

Sir William Walton at his home in Capri

William Walton was born at Oldham and became a boy chorister at Christchurch Cathedral, Oxford, before attending university there. Like Elgar, he was largely self-taught as a musician.

While at Oxford he received encouragement from the writers Osbert and Edith Sitwell to compose accompanying music for the recitation (through a mask with a megaphone!) of some of Edith Sitwell's poems. He later transformed this music into the ballet *Façade*. *Façade* remains one of Walton's most popular works, although the composer thought of it as no more than light-hearted humour in music. Osbert Sitwell also compiled the text for Walton's dramatic oratorio, *Belshazzar's Feast*, based on an episode from the book of Daniel.

Walton was knighted in 1951 and has spent much of his later life in the sunny Mediterranean island of Ischia.

Portsmouth Point is a light-hearted illustration in music based on a drawing by the 18th century cartoonist, Thomas Rowlandson. Rowlandson's drawing, as you can see, depicts the busy quay of Portsmouth harbour at the time of the Napoleonic Wars. Walton's overture has all the same excitement and variety of goings-on; it is a high-spirited piece with lots of bouncy rhythms. Written when the composer was only 23 years old, and first performed by the International Society for Contemporary Music in Zurich in 1926, *Portsmouth Point* is dedicated to the composer's friend, the poet Siegfried Sassoon.

The more you look at Rowlandson's drawing, the more you keep on discovering things you had not noticed before. See if you can spot details apart from those listed below.

1. Soldiers and sailors bound for the wars.
2. Fond farewells to wives and sweethearts.
3. People rolling barrels, carrying packs, humping sea chests.
4. Ships in the harbour, ready to set sail.
5. A line of washing hanging on a pole.
6. Underneath the washing line, the moneylender's shop. A queue of impatient customers waits outside.
7. On the right, the crowded Ship's Tavern.
8. In a doorway, a child pulling at her mother's skirts.
9. Above the doorway, a gentleman looks through a telescope.
10. A one-legged fiddler, trying to discourage the attentions of a stray dog, plays a merry tune.
11. People dancing, drinking and singing.
12. Dogs fighting.

GUIDE TO THE MUSIC

1. The first six bars of the overture introduce us to the bustle and activity of Portsmouth harbour. Although the full orchestra is playing most of the interest lies in the string parts.

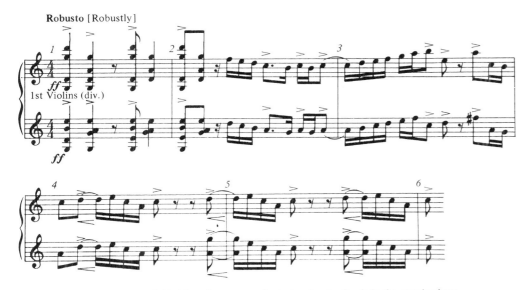

div. (divisi) = First violins divided into 2 groups, each playing 4-note chords in the opening bars.

2. At the start of bar 4 there is a semiquaver figure which recurs often throughout the piece. Try to remember its shape.

3. A broad, off-beat theme is announced Theme **A**.

This theme is in two parts, 'a' and 'b'. If you look carefully at the notes that go to make up these two sections of the theme you will notice that those of part 'b' occur in exactly the same order as in part 'a', but the rhythmic shape of part 'b' is subtly different from that of part 'a'. Composers often use repeated melodic shapes as points of reference. If you learn to recognise them as they occur, you will follow the music more easily. Walton takes this process a stage further by changing some of the melodic shapes of his music in the way we have seen in connection with Theme **A** and, if you listen carefully, you should be able to hear similar relationships elsewhere in his overture.

4. A quieter passage beings with this tune Theme **B**.

As you will see from the music quotation, this passage is written with continually changing numbers of beats in the bar. In the space of 12 bars the time signature changes 12 times and this feature gives the music its flexible character. This, together with the rising and falling repeated melodic phrases, could suggest the ebb and flow of the tide.

5. A temporary return to the music of the introduction is followed by Theme **A**, again altered rhythmically and played this time by violas and oboe.

6. The second main theme of the overture is heard again and the opening section of the overture is drawn to a close by a nautical reference — to the 'Sailor's Hornpipe'.

(Theme D)   Walton

Sailor's Hornpipe

7. Having introduced us to the main themes of his overture, Walton then goes on to develop some of these ideas. The middle section begins with reference to the introduction; new rhythmic figures soon appear, but there are also many variations of previous figures.

8. A new theme, Theme **E**, is introduced by clarinet and bass clarinet and is repeated by the bass of the whole orchestra.

(Theme E)

9. No new themes are introduced after this, so a brief description of what happens in the music should be enough to help you follow the remainder of the piece.

10. The semiquaver figure of bar 4 is used to build a short link passage.

1st Violins

11. It is followed by a trumpet variant of Theme **E**.

12. A climax is reached: Theme **E** is played by trombones, while the semi-quaver figure (from bar 4 of the overture) is played in canon between trumpet and strings; the violins play the same notes as the trumpet, but one beat later.

13. A shortened form of Theme **A** appears.

14. Theme **B** follows in a quiet version, and leads to

15. Theme **E**, played by trombones.

16. In the final bars, Theme **A** is played by the xylophone.

Sailors dancing a hornpipe

Cartoon of sailors enjoying themselves off-duty, by the 19th-century cartoonist George Cruickshank

The overture

As its name suggests, an overture was originally a piece of instrumental music which served as an introduction to an opera, oratorio, or similar piece. In the 17th century the function of an overture was frequently seen as no more than a kind of 'call to order' to attract the attention of the audience.

A much later development in the 19th century was the transfer of the overture from the opera house to the concert hall, and composers began to write independent pieces known as **concert overtures**. Walton's *Portsmouth Point*, therefore, follows a long tradition of works in this form which include Mendelssohn's *Fingal's Cave*, Berlioz's *Roman Carnival* and Brahms's *Academic Festival Overture* (see page 37).

⊏⟶ *FOLLOW UP*

It is hard to know whether Walton was consciously influenced by the melody shape of the sea shanty 'Johnny come down to Hilo' when writing the overture *Portsmouth Point*. But there is certainly a striking resemblance between the melodic shape of the chorus and Theme A in *Portsmouth Point*. Listen again to the overture and see how many times you can hear the chorus of the sea shanty in the music.

AN AMERICAN IN PARIS

ORCHESTRAL WORK
BY GEORGE GERSHWIN (1898-1937)

George Gershwin was born in Brooklyn, New York, in 1898 and died in Hollywood, California, in 1937. Although he became a famous pianist and composer in his later years, he came originally from a home where there were no opportunities to try out his musical talents. As a teenager he took piano lessons and got a job as piano-demonstrator at a shop in 'Tin Pan Alley'. With the publication of the song *Swanee*, which sold millions of copies,

Gershwin established himself as a force to be reckoned with in the field of light music, and about 1920 he began to develop his interest in jazz. *Rhapsody in Blue*, commissioned by the jazz musician Paul Whiteman, was Gershwin's first attempt at integrating the jazz idiom into a composition for piano and orchestra. It was a great success. Then came *An American in Paris*.

The Philharmonic Symphony Orchestra of New York under their conductor Walter Damrosch evidently conveyed with relish the carefree good humour of the piece; the first-night audience responded rapturously. The music was easy to listen to, tuneful, with jazzy rhythms and instrumental effects. No sooner was the piece over than the audience directed their thunderous applause to Gershwin, sitting in a box surrounded by family and friends. Since its first performance the piece has been turned into a ballet (Gershwin originally described as a rhapsodic ballet) and in 1951 was made into an Academy Award-winning film starring Gene Kelly and Lesley Caron.

This is how Gershwin saw his own writing in relation to the 'folk music' of America — in this case jazz:

Jazz

To understand the relationship of Gershwin's music to jazz, we need to know something about its origins. Jazz has its roots in community music-making, stretching back to the days of slavery, when negroes were brought over from Africa to work on the cotton plantations of the southern states of America. Slaves played banjos, fiddles, and guitars, and after the Civil War (1861-1865) acquired trumpets, trombones, and clarinets discarded by the armies. The music was not written down and always contained a large amount of improvisation. But although its origins were much older, jazz didn't really become popular as a musical form until the 1890's when groups of musicians got together in the busy port at the mouth of the Mississippi — New Orleans. By the beginning of this century it had reached New York, with New Yorkers enjoying music describing life on the old plantations, performed not by negroes but by white men who blacked their faces. Minstrel-style shows which caricatured negro life were also all the rage in London. However, New York did have a jazz piano style of its own which was a mixture of Ragtime and Blues — two other elements which run through jazz.

By the mid 1920's some of the best New Orleans musicians had moved north to Chicago. Paul Whiteman was the 'King of Jazz' in this period and the music was beginning to be recognised as a serious art form. The big commercial breakthrough, however, did not come until the 1930's; young white Americans were seized by a passion for dancing, and the music was supplied by 'swing' bands. Against this background, Gershwin produced such compositions as *Rhapsody in Blue* (1924, composed for Paul Whiteman), his *Piano Concerto in F* (1925), his folk-opera *Porgy and Bess* (1935), and *An American in Paris*. In his music you will find elements of popular and serious music happily existing side by side.

The great music of the past in other countries has always been built on folk-music (music of the people for the people); America is no exception. Jazz, Ragtime, Negro Spiritual and Blues, Southern mountain songs, country fiddling, and cowboy songs can all be employed in the creation of an American art-music ('serious' music). Jazz I regard as an American folk-music ... I believe that it can be made the basis of serious symphonic works of lasting value, in the hands of a composer with talent for both jazz and symphonic music.

GUIDE TO THE MUSIC

For the first performance on 13 December 1928, at Carnegie Hall, the composer prepared detailed comments which are paraphrased here.

'Imagine an American, visiting Paris, swinging down the Champs-Elysées on a mild, sunny morning in May or June. He is off at full speed at once, to the tune of The First Walking Theme, a straightforward tune, designed to convey an impression of French freedom and gaiety.'

First Walking Theme

The American notes with pleasure the sounds of the city. French taxi-cabs seem to amuse him particularly, a fact that the orchestra points out in a brief episode introducing four Parisian taxi horns. These have a special theme given to them which is announced by the strings whenever they appear in the score.

Sul G = on the G string, an indication to all the violin players to perform the notes under the dotted bracket on the G string of their instruments; this gives a rich, warm tone.

Having safely avoided the taxis, our American passes the open door of a cafe, through which you can hear *La Sorella* (the name of a song popular in the 1900's) played on the trombones.

Exhilarated by this reminder of the gay 1900s, he resumes his stroll. The Second Walking Theme is announced by the clarinet 'in French with a strong American accent', as Gershwin puts it.

Second Walking Theme

Both themes are now discussed at some length by the instruments, until our tourist happens to pass something, perhaps a church or the *Grand Palais*. The American respectfully slackens his pace as he passes them. Listen for the sober theme played on the cor anglais.

At this point the American's route becomes somewhat obscured. When the Third Walking Theme makes its eventual appearance our American has crossed the Seine and is somewhere on the Left Bank.

Third Walking Theme

The Third Walking Theme is less French than its predecessors, in keeping with the fact that there are always lots of foreigners, especially Americans, on the Left Bank. The theme becomes progressively slower. The end of this section of the work is blurred, suggesting that the American is on the *terrasse* of a cafe, exploring the mysteries of an *Anise de Lozo* (a drink).

Pavement café in Paris in the 1930s

And now the orchestra introduces a sleazy episode. A woman (solo violin) approaches our hero and speaks to him in charming broken English; the one-sided conversation continues for a time.

Our hero becomes homesick. He has the Blues; notice how the orchestra conveys his gloomy mood.

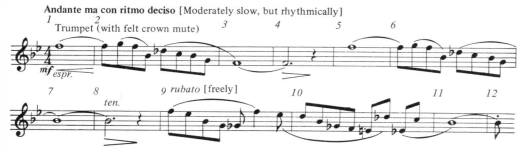

He realises suddenly that he does not belong to this place and that he is nothing but a foreigner. The cool blue Paris sky, the distant upward sweep of the Eiffel Tower, the book-stalls on the quay, the pattern of horse chestnut leaves on the white sun-flecked streets — what does it all matter? He longs to be back in the world he knows best, home.

The orchestra rescues him with a theme introduced by two trumpets. Our hero meets a fellow American, the piece ends with a noisy, cheerful, self-confident Charleston, without a drop of French blood in its veins.

For the moment, Paris is forgotten. The orchestra represents the wise-cracking of the two Americans. Walking Theme number two enters soon, enthusiastically supported by number three. Paris isn't such a bad place after all. The Blues

returns, but it is a happy reminiscence rather than a homesick yearning, and the orchestra, in a riotous finale, decides to make a night of it. The Americans decide to enjoy Paris while they can.

WHAT THE CRITICS SAID

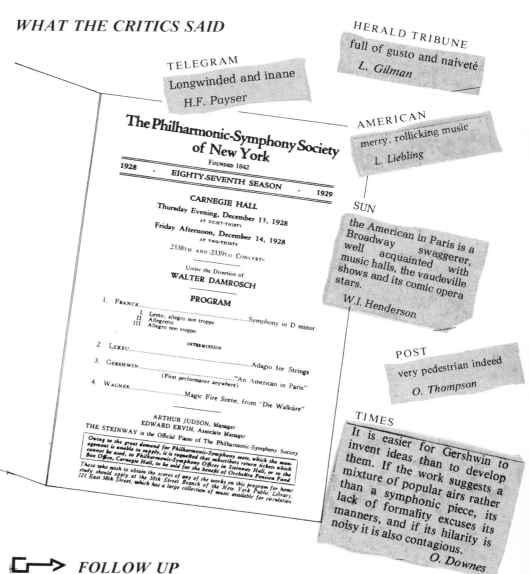

➡ *FOLLOW UP*

Discuss the views of the critics and then try to make up a short review for a newspaper saying what *you* think of the piece.

WASHINGTON'S BIRTHDAY

ORCHESTRAL PIECE

BY CHARLES IVES (1874-1954)

The New England town of Newhaven, Connecticut, in the early 20th century

Charles Ives is often called the 'father of American music', but his music has, until now, been largely neglected. Born in Danbury, Connecticut, in 1874, he was long regarded as a musical eccentric. He studied music as a boy with his father (also a musician), and loved to experiment with new musical styles.

When he entered Yale University he was more interested in baseball than his studies as an organist and, after graduating, he was more successful as a businessman than as a composer. He believed artists could make a living without giving up their artistic ideals. As a result he dedicated himself to building one of the great insurance sales agencies of America. His musical composition was done in the hours he could spare from 'Ives and Myrick', and as his business prospered he invested his profits in printing and publishing his own music and putting on performances of it.

The heavy demands of business and artistic life caused early illness, and Ives spent the last half of his life in retirement as a semi-invalid.

The music of Charles Ives is a scrapbook of American life at the beginning of the 20th century. Ives took the evangelical hymns, the popular melodies of the dance-hall, the military band marches, the sounds of village life, and college songs, and wove them into his compositions in a strikingly original way.

Washington's Birthday, composed in 1909, was one of four scores which Ives placed in a folder labelled 'Four New England Holidays, recollections of a boy's holidays in a Connecticut country town. These movements may be played as separate pieces or may be lumped together as a symphony.'

The piece is scored for a chamber orchestra consisting of strings, one horn, one flute, a set of bells and a Jew's harp (if available). The first part of this piece conveys the picture of a dismal, bleak, cold February night near New Fairfield. It is the time of year when the anniversary of the birth of George Washington falls.

The music has a timeless quality, as though it has been frozen into immobility. At the end of his score Ives quotes a poem *Snow-Bound*, which begins:

The moon above the eastern wood
Shone at its full; the hill-range stood
Transfigured in the silver flood . . .

George Washington

George Washington, the first President of the United States of America, was born on 22 February 1732, and the anniversary of his birth is celebrated each year in the United States with a national holiday (the fourth Monday of February).

GUIDE TO THE MUSIC

You may be surprised to recognise the beginning of *Home, sweet home*

and a snatch of *Old folks at home*.

The music continues in the mood of the opening for some time, like a camera panning slowly across a snow-covered vista, and the image gradually fades. Snatches of *Turkey in the straw* and the *Sailor's Hornpipe* are heard in anticipation of the barn dance music which follows.

The violins strike up a merry dance tune and the atmosphere is completely transformed. The barn dance is made up of tunes and songs of the day (some humorous, some sentimental, and some serious) but, because of the strange way they are combined, the effect is something new. Ives remembered some of these dances from his boyhood, and also remembers his father's descriptions of the old dancing and fiddle-playing. In some parts of the hall a group would be dancing the polka, while in another a waltz, with perhaps another dance going on in the middle of the room. Some of the players in the band would join in with the polka and some with the waltz. Sometimes the change in tempo and mixed rhythms would be caused by a performer who was getting a little sleepy after three or four hours solid playing, and at other times by a player who had been drinking too much.

The music of the barn dance is like a montage picture which is built up in sound, layer upon layer. Here are the tunes Ives uses.

The White Cockade combined with *Massa's in de Cold Ground*

Turkey in the Straw (Old Zip Coon)

A barn dance

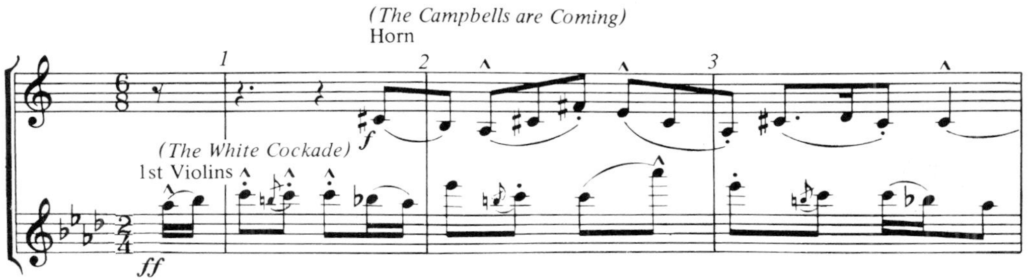
(The Campbells are Coming)
Horn
(The White Cockade)
1st Violins
ff

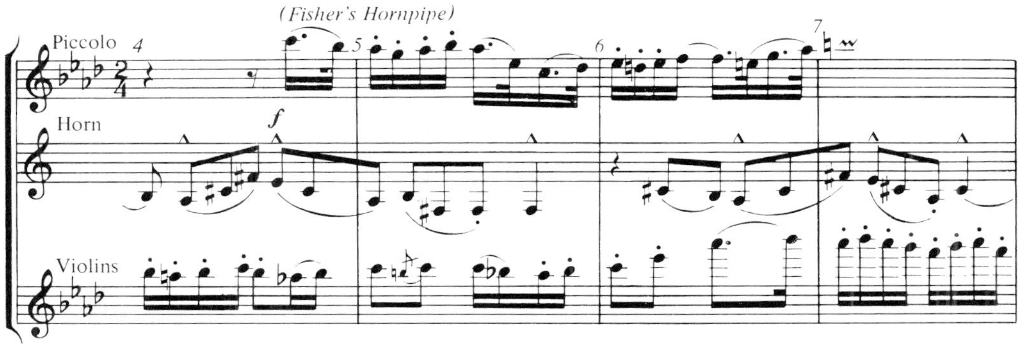
(Fisher's Hornpipe)
Piccolo
Horn
Violins

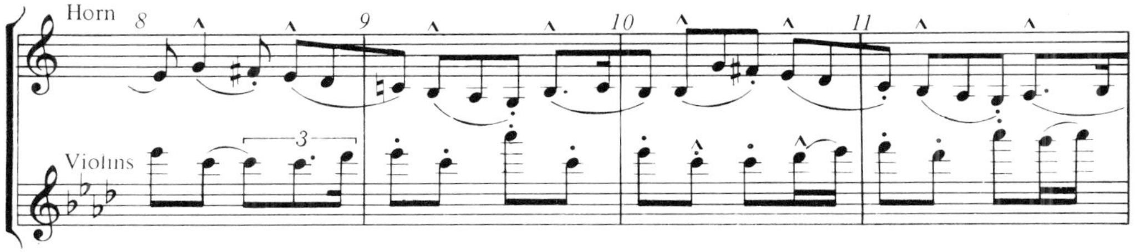
Horn
Violins

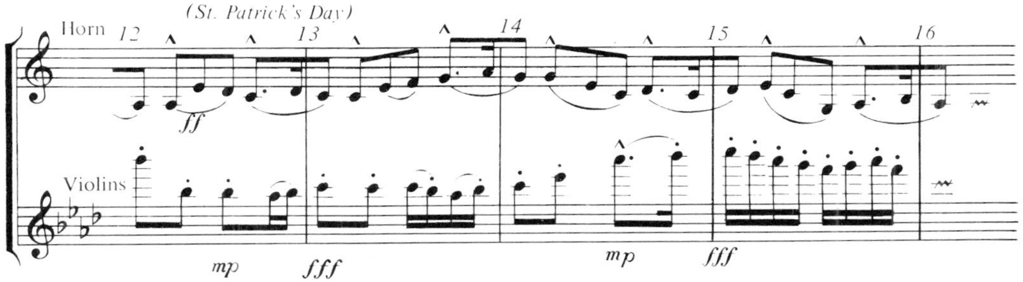
(St. Patrick's Day)
Horn
Violins
ff
mp
fff

As the festivities draw to a close the mood passes through various stages from the high-spirited entry of the Jew's harp (a large number of Jew's harps are necessary since one could not be heard at all) to a romantic Viennese waltz. At the old barn dances almost all the men would carry Jew's harps in their waistcoat pockets or in the calves of their boots, and several would stand around on the side of the dance floor and play the harp more as a drum than as a melody instrument since it can't really play a tune. The slower section which follows includes a solitary fiddler playing *Pig Town Fling*.

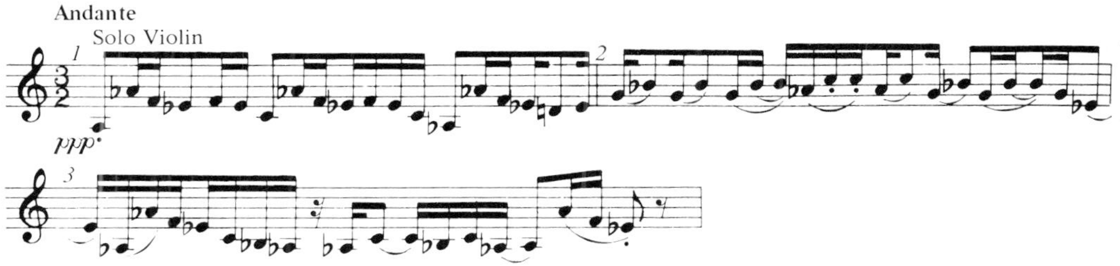
Andante
Solo Violin
ppp

This is followed by *Turkey in the straw*. A chorus of *Good night, ladies*

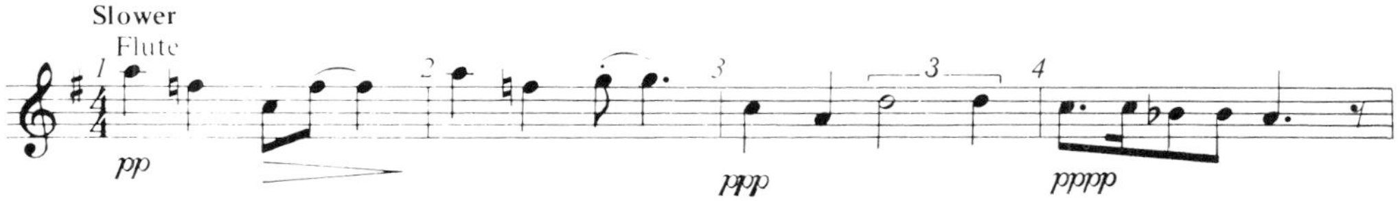
Slower
Flute
pp
ppp
pppp

dissolves into the rhythmic breathing of sleep at the end of a day of celebration, energetically enjoyed.

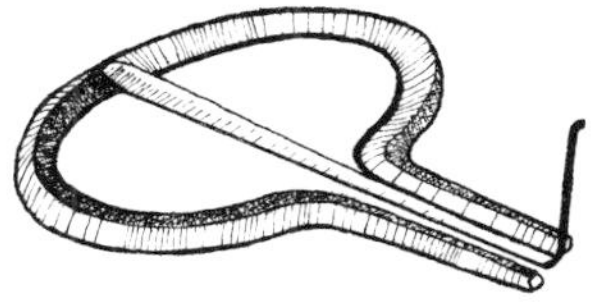

A Jew's harp

FOLLOW UP

Many of the songs used in Ives's score can be found in the *Oxford Song Book* (O.U.P.); learn to sing them and 'spot' them when you listen again to *Washington's Birthday*.

Water Music

SUITE

BY GEORGE FRIDERIC HANDEL (1685-1759)

Born in Halle (Germany) in 1685, Handel grew up to become a skilled performer on organ, harpsichord, violin and oboe and also a gifted composer in his own right. For a time he was employed as Kapellmeister (musician in charge of court music) to the Elector of Hanover, who later became George I, king of England. In 1710 he visited London where he was welcomed for his outstanding gifts both as composer and performer; shortly afterwards Handel settled down to live in England where he stayed for the remainder of his life. When his former employer became king of England, Handel was engaged as music-master to the royal family.

For a time it was believed that the *Water Music* was responsible for bringing about a reconciliation between Handel and George I. George, as Elector of Hanover, reacted angrily to his Kapellmeister's long absence in London and when appointed king was reported to have refused to communicate further with Handel. But Handel regained the king's favour through writing the *Water Music*. The story is highly plausible, but probably quite untrue.

The river Thames in the early 18th century was one of the main highways of London. Each summer, many passenger boats were hailed by people (much in the same way as we today might hail a taxi) from piers along the river's banks. Also to be seen on the river were many private barges luxuriously fitted out and manned by liveried servants. A favourite pastime of early 18th-century London society was to make up a water party on the Thames with a band of musicians in attendance.

George I particularly liked the atmosphere of the Thames and, with the court close by the river at Whitehall,

Whitehall and Horse Guards' Parade in Handel's time

there were many water parties to Hampton Court or Richmond; often the royal barge was accompanied by a boat-load of musicians who entertained the royal party for the duration of their outing.

The *Daily Courant* of 19 July 1717 describes a typical water party on the Thames.

> On Wednesday evening (July 17) at about eight the King took water at Whitehall in an open barge . . .wherein were also the Duchess of Bolton, the Duchess of Newcastle, the Countess of Godolphin, Madam Kilmanseck, and the Earl of Orkney, and went up the river towards Chelsea. Many other barges with persons of quality attended, and so great a number of boats, that the whole river in a manner was covered.
>
> A City Company's barge was employed for the music, wherein were fifty instruments of all sorts, who played all the way from Lambeth, while the barges drove with the tide without rowing as far as Chelsea, the finest symphonies, composed express for this occasion by Mr. Hendel, which His Majesty liked so well that he caused it to be played over three times in going and returning. At eleven his Majesty went ashore at Chelsea, where a supper was prepared, and then there was another very fine

> consort of music, which lasted till two, after which His Majesty came again into his barge and returned the same way, the music continuing to play until he landed.

The instruments on the barge included trumpets, horns, oboes, bassoons, flutes, recorders and strings. Each performance lasted an hour and there were two performances before supper and one after. The cost of the orchestra was £150. The composer mentioned in the report is George Frideric Handel (Hendel was the way the English spelled his name) and the piece of music is his celebrated *Water Music*.

The *Water Music* was published in 1741 and consisted of 25 pieces, some of which had been written (probably for other water parties) before or after that date. Present-day concert performances and recordings of the *Water Music* are sometimes given in an arrangement with orchestration by Sir Hamilton Harty. His version of the suite includes five movements: Overture, Air, Bourrée, Hornpipe, and Finale.

GUIDE TO THE MUSIC

1. Overture

Perhaps the most striking thing about this movement is the way in which Handel opposes the tone colour of the horns to that of the strings and woodwind combined. This contrast of tone colour is quite unusual in 18th-century music, where composers tended to choose one colour for a movement and retain that colour throughout.

One other point which may have struck you is the relatively small range of notes used by the horns. In Handel's day players did not have the benefit of valves to produce a wide variety of notes.

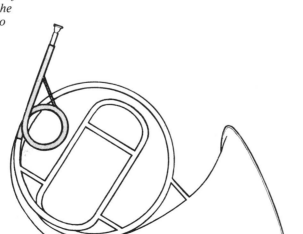

An 18th-century crook horn showing, shaded, the detachable crook. A wider range of notes could be obtained by the use of different sized crooks which altered the length of tubing, and players learnt to change these crooks very quickly.

2. Air

A feature of this movement is the frequency with which you will hear its opening phrase. It occurs on not less than 12 occasions if all the repeats are played. Within the phrase itself there is also a degree of repetition since the second bar uses the same motif (♩ ♫ ♫ ♩) as the first, and bar 3 resumes the dotted element of the opening motif.

3. Bourrée

A dance of probably French or Spanish origin, the Bourrée was first 'invented' about 1600. With two minim beats in the bar, each phrase of this lively dance begins on the last crotchet. The Bourrée has a quite distinct character of its own.

4. Hornpipe

Before you listen to this piece look at the single-stave guide and try to follow the development of the rhythmic motif of the opening bar throughout the movement.

The melody can be broken up into these fragments:
The first phrase consisting of bars 1 and 2.
The rhythm of bar 1 is repeated in bar 3.
The same again occurs in bar 4.
Bars 5 and 6 are an exact repetition of the first phrase.
Bar 7 contains an important and exciting displacement of the accent.
Bar 9 begins as the first phrase, but 10 makes a reference back to the rhythmic displacement in bar 7.

To increase interest, Handel (in bar 11) changes the order of crotchets and pairs of quavers which first appeared in bar 2 as ♩ ♫ and now appear in the more emphatic form ♫ ♩.
Bar 13 resembles bar 1, but retains the emphatic pairs of quavers on the beat. Bars 15 and 16 round off the movement, the last bar having the same rhythm as the last bar of the first section.

5. Finale

As you listen to this piece jot down the number of occasions on which you hear the distinctive opening of this movement.

The middle section of the movement has an altogether quieter and sadder feeling than the opening. This is reflected not only in the absence of the brass instruments with their associations of festivity but also in the change from major to minor key, i.e. the change from 'happy' to 'sad'. The boisterous mood of the *allegro*, however, resumes and the opening section is repeated. This simple musical form can be represented by the letters ABA.

The palace of Hampton Court in the 18th century

Handel wrote a great many **oratorios** *(religious words set to music for solo singers, chorus, and orchestra). Messiah is one of his most famous oratorios. This engraving shows Handel conducting an oratorio.*

A river party on the Thames, by the English painter Zoffany

The suite

The 18th century suite consisted of a succession of contrasting dance movements. In the instrumental suites of Handel and J. S. Bach the four most popular dance types were:

I **Allemande** of German origin; moderate speed; generally with an up-beat beginning

II **Courante** a lively 'running' dance in 3 time; French or Italian versions

III **Sarabande** a slow, stately dance in 3 time with a characteristic accent on the second beat of three, e.g.

IV **Gigue** a lively, quick movement; of English or Irish origin; usually the finale of the suite.

⇨ *FOLLOW UP*

1. Try to describe a movement of the *Water Music* e.g. The 'Bourrée'. The description of the 'Air' on the previous page will help you to tackle this question.

2. Listen to a suite by Handel or J. S. Bach which contains these four basic movements. One of those listed below might give you a start.

G. F. Handel *Suite No. 4 in E minor (Vol. 1) for harpsichord*

Suite No. 4 in D minor (Vol. 2) for harpsichord

J. S. Bach *French Suite No. 6 in E major for harpsichord*

Suite in B minor for flute and strings

ANSWERS TO 'QUIZ', QUESTIONS 8 AND 9

8. La donna è mobile (Rigoletto): Goodbye Old Paint (Billy the Kid): Fox's Song (Academic Festival Overture): Johnny come down to Hilo (Portsmouth Point).
9. Till Eulenspiegel: Dorabella: Portsmouth Point: Oh what's the porter got?: The Blues: St. Patrick's Day.

4. Spot the 'odd man out'.

(a)	(b)	(c)	(d)	(e)
Rossini	Guitar	Oboe	*Portsmouth Point*	*Andante*
Verdi	Fluviol	Flute	*Academic Festival*	*Allegro*
Puccini	Zampoña	Clarinet	*Romeo and Juliet*	*Presto*
Albéniz	Cimbalom	French horn	*Háry János*	*Con sordini*

1. Solve these anagrams. They are all instruments you have met in this book.

SBSONOA   ORC GLASINA
NCEFRH ORHN   UGTRAI
MMCBAOLI   LFVLOIU

2. Which composer and which music?

An American composer of popular ballets / a suite about a cowboy shot by his friend
An English composer who collected folk songs / a symphony based on film music
A friend of Queen Victoria / a symphony inspired by a Scottish journey
An American business man / a collection of songs and tunes about New England
A leading 20th century Russian composer / orchestral piece about a 17th century peasant rebellion

3. a) Fill in the gaps in these musical terms.

p - - z - - - -   - - is - - - - -
- - v - s -   r - - - r - - - d -
- n - - n - -   - - - in - - nd -

b) Put the right meanings beside each word.

at a walking pace; getting slower; plucked; getting softer; divided; slide.

5. Match the following columns in pairs.

The Duke	Soprano	Woodwind	Xylophone
Rigoletto	Bass	Brass	Trombone
Sparafucile	Tenor	Strings	Cor anglais
Gilda	Baritone	Percussion	Viola

f	getting louder	Portsmouth	Copland
p	loud	Scotland	Walton
	accent	Lincoln County	Handel
>	soft, quiet	River Thames	Mendelssohn

6. Arrange the following lists in chronological order.

Composers:	*Works:*
Shostakovich	*Enigma Variations*
Brahms	*Sinfonia Antartica*
Mendelssohn	*Rigoletto*
Handel	*Romeo and Juliet*

7. Place the following lists of instruments in order from highest to lowest.

Viola, Violin, Double Bass, 'Cello
Clarinet, Flute, Bassoon, Oboe
Trombone, Tuba, French horn, Trumpet